BRAHMS

THE CONCERTGOER'S COMPANIONS

SERIES EDITOR ALEC HYATT KING

BRAHMS

A biography with a survey
of books, editions & recordings

by

KATHLEEN DALE

CLIVE BINGLEY LONDON

FIRST PUBLISHED 1970 BY CLIVE BINGLEY LTD
16 PEMBRIDGE ROAD W11
SET IN 10 ON 13 POINT LINOTYPE TIMES
AND PRINTED IN THE UK BY
THE CENTRAL PRESS (ABERDEEN) LTD
COPYRIGHT © KATHLEEN DALE 1970
ALL RIGHTS RESERVED
85157 101 8

CONTENTS

For assistance in obtaining material for study I am deeply indebted to the Music Room of the British Museum, to the librarians of the Central Music Library, Westminster, and of the German Institute in London, to the Suffolk County Librarian, Ipswich, the branch librarians at Beccles and Southwold, and to Dr Hans Gal, Edinburgh.

KATHLEEN DALE

Brahms's life

ANCESTRY AND BOYHOOD: In the year 1826 a north German peasant of nineteen, one Johann Jakob Brahms, from the lower Elbe region of Holstein, made his way into Hamburg to seek his fortune as a musician. His father, an innkeeper and retailer in the village of Heide, had intended that his son should follow in his own footsteps, but the boy had early decided to be a musician and would not be gainsaid. He even ran away from home several times in the attempt to obtain tuition in playing. His father finally saw that opposition was useless. He allowed Johann Jakob to be apprenticed to an institution in the neighbourhood where guild musicians were trained as orchestral players with a view to performing music for dances, weddings and sundry festive occasions. At the end of five years, having become proficient in playing violin, viola, cello, flute and horn, Johann received his indenture and left his village to pursue a career in the nearest big city.

On arrival in Hamburg, with only slender means at his disposal, he had to make do with lodgings in the most squalid and least reputable part of the city, the sailors' quarter, where he soon found humble employment playing in dance saloons and taverns. Within a few years he had progressed so far as to be appointed one of the hornists in a battalion of the town guard: a position which gave him both the right to wear a smart uniform, and the financial security he needed to set up a home of his own. In 1830 he married in Hamburg Johanna Henrike Christiane Nissen, a skilled needle-woman, in humble circumstances though of much more cultivated ancestry than his own. She was his senior by seventeen years, not robust in health and slightly lame, but an excellent housewife, sweet

7

and affectionate by nature. Three children were born to this strangely assorted couple; first a daughter, Elizabeth (Elise) and then two sons, the elder of whom was the composer Johannes Brahms, and the younger, Friedrich (Fritz), also a musician, generally known later as ' the wrong Brahms '.

At the time of Johannes' birth on May 7 1833, the family was living in the first floor dwelling of no 60 Speckstrasse, a picturesque old timber framed house, which stood until it was destroyed by bombing 110 years later. After the younger son was born in 1835 they moved to slightly more spacious quarters, still in the same poverty-stricken district, where Frau Brahms set up a tiny business in haberdashery to eke out her husband's scanty earnings. He, in the meantime, had learned to play the double bass, on which instrument he eventually became a regular player in the band at the Alster Pavilion, which performed programmes of light music every evening throughout the year.

Johannes passed his childhood in a musical atmosphere and showed his own gifts at an early age. When he was about four years old his father began to teach him the violin and cello, but as soon as the child heard a piano he longed to be allowed to study this instrument rather than strings. He also made some attempts at composition. He was seven and already a schoolboy when he was taken by his father to Otto Cossel, an excellent and conscientious local piano teacher who undertook his musical training. Johannes, who was by nature studious and hard working, made such rapid progress with his playing that at the end of three years Cossel felt that he had little more to teach him and would have liked to transfer him to the more expert care of his own former teacher Edward Marxsen, at Altona, a suburb of Hamburg. But Marxsen was not yet willing to accept him.

Just at this time, the ten year old Johannes made his first public appearance as a pianist at a concert in Hamburg arranged for his benefit. He took part in performances of Beethoven's quintet for wind instruments and piano, and in a Mozart piano quartet, and played some solos. The concert was so successful that Jakob now felt justified in approaching Marxsen personally to beg him to accept Johannes as a pupil. Marxsen consented, though only to a

8

limited extent, promising to give Johannes one lesson a week on condition that he still continued his tuition with Cossel.

At the concert just mentioned an impresario happened to be present. He was so deeply impressed by Johannes' playing that he asked Jakob to let him take the boy on tour in America as a prodigy, promising that he would earn large sums of money. Jakob, overjoyed at the prospect of financial plenty, broke the dazzling news to Cossel, who immediately sensed the danger of exposing the immature Johannes to commercial exploitation. He hastened to Marxsen and implored him to decide on becoming solely responsible for Johannes' musical education. This time he won his way. Johannes became a fulltime pupil of the more widely cultivated musician, who would take no payment for his services and whose influence was decisive for the whole of Johannes' subsequent musical career. It was Marxsen, not Cossel, who first recognised his potential as a composer and who started him off with instruction in theory, counterpoint and harmony, and who encouraged him to study the finest music of the classical and early periods (although he would not allow his pupils to play Schumann and Chopin). He also stimulated the boy's passion for reading serious literature by lending him a steady flow of books.

Johannes had begun his general education when he was six, attending first one small private school and going on to another when he was ten. In addition to the usual school subjects he learned sufficient English and French to be able to read, though not to speak these two languages. His own voracious reading, which he continued all his life, was the principal source of the wide general culture he eventually acquired. Even in boyhood, all his few spare coins were spent on books, and he eagerly borrowed any that were available to him.

The poverty of the Brahms family during the 1840's was so acute that Johannes' parents were not unwilling to let him help to earn some money by playing dance music nightly in poor class local saloons. This uncongenial task became a great strain on the boy's health; he began to suffer from anemia and to need fresh air and relaxation. His father then asked one of his patrons, Herr Giese-mann, a paper-mill owner and farmer who lived in the country not

9

far from Hamburg, if he would invite Johannes to spend a few weeks at his home; the boy, in return, would supply any musical services that the family might require. Johannes accordingly spent part of the summer of 1847 with the kindly family at Winsen an der Luhe, coming back to Hamburg each week by steamboat for his music lessons. His health was restored by the open air life he led, swimming in the river and walking in the woods. He enjoyed happy companionship with Giesemann's little daughter Lischen, who was a year younger than himself. They shared a love of reading and he gave her piano lessons. Perhaps most important of all, he gained his first experience of composing for and conducting a small male voice choir, the Winsen Choral Society. He also enjoyed opportunities for playing duet arrangements of some of Beethoven's works with a district bailiff resident in the neighbourhood, Herr Blume, who invited him to his house to practise on his piano and to play with him. Incidentally, with Lischen Johannes made acquaintance with Tieck's story of *The beautiful Magelone and the Knight Peter*, fifteen poems from which formed the basis of his song cycle *Magelone lieder* op 33, composed in the 1860's.

BOYHOOD'S END

Johannes resumed his routine of study in Hamburg during the autumn and winter of 1847-48, also playing at one or two concerts and acquiring a very small measure of local fame. In the summer of 1848, after finishing his school education, he was again at Winsen for a short time on a friendly visit. For the choral society that year he arranged two folksongs, thus early evincing that partiality for utilising his native folkmusic which he was to show all through his career. Returning to Hamburg in the autumn he gave his first public concert, with assistance from other local musicians. In addition to performing some undistinguished pieces, which were doubtless chosen to accord with the public taste of the day, Johannes dared to play a Bach fugue. At his second concert, in the spring of 1849, he was even bold enough to include Beethoven's 'Waldstein' sonata, as well as a 'Fantasia for piano on a favourite waltz' of his own composition. The last named item was one of a whole series of *pot-pourris* and transcriptions of light music which Johannes and other composers were commissioned by the Hamburg publisher Cranz to contribute to his catalogue under the composite name of ' G W Marks '. This hack work, together with the giving of piano lessons at very cheap rates, the nightly employment in the dance saloons and occasional engagements as accompanist were the young musician's only sources of income. In his free time he was hard at work composing. He used to practise regularly at a piano shop in Hamburg and in so doing met a slightly older local pianist, Louise Japha. She took a keen interest in his work and tried to introduce him to the music of Robert Schumann, who, with his wife Clara, paid a visit to Hamburg in 1850. Johannes sent some of his compositions to Schumann's hotel for the composer's criticism, but the parcel was returned to him unopened—a rebuff Johannes did not lightly forget, although it did not stem the flow of his inspiration. Among the many works he composed during the years 1851-52 were the scherzo in E flat minor, the whole of the piano sonata in F sharp minor and the beginning of the sonata in C. But as a composer of serious music Johannes was still unpublished and unknown to the music public, both in Hamburg and beyond. It happened that a turn in world events was to set him on the path towards recognition.

The revolutionary disturbances which broke out in Germany and Austria in 1848 caused a number of refugees to flee to Hamburg during the early 1850's, whence many eventually sailed to America. Among them was a contingent of Hungarians who remained in the city for some time. One of these, Edward Reményi, a virtuoso violinist of partly Jewish descent, who had been a fellow student of Joseph Joachim's in Vienna, gave some concerts, for one of which Johannes was engaged as the accompanist. Reményi, who was three years older than Johannes, was so delighted with his musicianly playing, and Johannes in turn was so strongly stimulated by Reményi's spirited performance of his native Hungarian music, that the two played together on several occasions. The Hungarians as a body were eventually expelled from Hamburg by the police as politically dangerous, but Reményi somehow managed to return before the end of the year, and he then resumed his collaboration with Johannes.

11

Early in 1853 Reményi and Johannes worked up a programme, which included Beethoven's sonata in C minor for violin and piano and Vieuxtemps' violin concerto in E, for performance at Winsen, where they were strongly supported by Johannes' circle of friends in that neighbourhood. In the audience was the music-loving district bailiff Herr Blume with whom Johannes had formerly played duets. He now suggested that the concert might be repeated in two north German towns, Celle and Lüneburg, where he could use his influence in favour of the performers. This idea led to the planning of a concert tour that would also include Hanover. There, Reményi could count on the interest of Joseph Joachim, who held an appointment at the court.

In April the pair of musicians set out on their journey, Johannes taking with him the manuscripts of his latest compositions. He was not quite twenty and in some ways young for his years; boyish in appearance, with a mane of fair hair, brilliantly blue eyes and a high pitched voice. He felt the parting from his parents keenly, for he was devoted to his bluff, good natured father and his sensitive, loving mother, and they to him. He made his mother promise to write him a long letter every week—a promise she faithfully kept although it was not easy for her. Johannes, to whom letter writing was less of a burden, sent home long accounts of the exciting happenings in the succeeding months.

At the first concert, at Celle, the only piano available for the occasion was found at the last minute to be a semitone below pitch. Reményi was unwilling to tune his violin down to accord with it, but Johannes saved the situation by transposing his piano parts a semitone upwards. He himself made light of this remarkable feat of musicianship but it created a mild sensation. After the next two equally successful concerts at Lüneburg, where Johannes also played part of his C major sonata at a private soirée (without arousing any particular enthusiasm), the musicians returned to Celle for one more concert. Then came the visit to Hanover, which for Johannes proved to be a landmark in the tour; for here he made the personal acqaintance of Joachim and so laid the foundation of a friendship which

12

was destined to enrich the lives of each of them, both musically and personally.

Joseph Joachim, at twenty three, was already in the very front rank as a violinist, as well as being an accomplished composer and conductor. On hearing Johannes play from his manuscripts he at once recognised in the shy youth a composer of great originality and promise. He perceived, too, that the musically unequal partnership between Johannes and Reményi was unlikely to endure, so he quietly took the opportunity of telling Johannes that if he needed help at the end of the concert tour he might go to join him in Göttingen where he would be living during the summer. Meanwhile a recommendation from him secured the pair an engagement to play before King George of Hanover and the court circle. Immediately after this concert, the police, having heard of Reményi's supposed revolutionary proclivities, ordered the partners to leave Hanover at once. Joachim had already given them an introduction to Liszt at Weimar, whither they travelled straightaway.

At Weimar they received an invitation from Liszt, who was living in the Altenburg, the magnificent house of Princess Caroline von Sayn Wittgenstein, surrounded by pupils, admirers and members of the so called ' New German ' school, whose musical ideals were in strong contrast to the strictly classical principles in which Johannes had been nurtured by Cossel and Marxsen. Johannes was overcome by shyness in this glittering assembly and even though he was pressed by both Liszt and Reményi to play some of his compositions, he could not face the ordeal. Liszt settled the difficulty himself by playing the scherzo in E flat minor and part of the sonata in C at sight with the utmost ease. He also gave Johannes some advice on one of his unfinished compositions and then, by request, played his own sonata in B minor to the company. But although Johannes was grateful to Liszt for his kindness, liked him personally and was full of admiration for his miraculous playing, he did not admire his compositions. Moreover, he felt a complete stranger in an artificial world which was far removed from his own humble home background. He was out of his element altogether and longed to escape. On the other hand, the superficially brilliant Reményi found his spiritual home in Liszt's circle and wished to remain in Weimar.

The partnership between the two had been growing uneasy, because Johannes seemed, unconsciously, to be attracting the greater share of attention. Now, it inevitably came to an end. Johannes left Weimar, alone, for Göttingen.

The two never met again, but the Hungarian style and spirit of some of Brahms's compositions undoubtedly sprang from the influence exerted upon him by Reményi during his formative years.

INTERLUDE

Joachim was attending courses in history and philosophy at the University of Göttingen when Johannes joined him late in June. During the next few weeks a radiantly happy companionship was established between the two young men, who shared similar artistic aims but whose early experiences up to this point had been widely contrasted—Joachim's a series of resounding successes, Johannes' a long hard struggle. They made music together, discussed and criticised each other's compositions and exchanged reminiscences of their earlier days. Although Johannes did not actually attend any lectures, he joined in the recreational activities of Joachim's circle of student acquaintances. Time passed rapidly. In August the two friends gave a concert in Göttingen which brought in welcome funds. Johannes could now carry out a much cherished wish to go for a walking tour along the Rhine. At the end of the month he parted from Joachim, cheered by the prospect of meeting him again in October in Hanover, and armed with a little sheaf of his visiting cards for use as passports to interesting musicians upon whom he might call during his wanderings. But even Joachim was not able to persuade him to decide definitely to visit Schumann at Düsseldorf.

Early in September Johannes reached Bonn, where he called on J W von Wasielevsky, a violinist and composer who later became one of Schumann's biographers. He listened sympathetically to Johannes playing his compositions and suggested that he should make the acquaintance of the Deichmann family at Mehlem, not far away across the Rhine. They were patrons of music and the arts, at whose house promising young aspirants, as well as celebrities, were always welcomed. The Deichmanns were delighted to receive Johannes as a friend of Joachim's and invited him to spend some time with them. During his stay he played his compositions, including the now completed sonata in C and some songs, to an interested circle of musicians among whom was the well-known pianist and conductor Franz Wüllner. He made excursions on foot in the beautiful country surrounding Mehlem and began to think out his sonata in F minor. And it was at the Deichmanns that he first had the opportunity of hearing and studying Schumann's compositions, so few of which were already known to him. Now, at last, it was borne in upon Johannes how nearly his own musical ideals and romantic tendencies coincided with Schumann's. He was overjoyed to discover, incidentally, that Schumann had drawn inspiration from two German romantic writers whom he himself had loved from boyhood, E T A Hoffmann and Jean Paul Richter. In Schumann's ' Kreisleriana ', Johannes rediscovered one of his own heroes, Kapellmeister Kreisler, in admiration for whom he had already adopted the pseudonym ' Young Kreisler ' as the signature to his sonata in F sharp minor.

Johannes was no longer in any doubt about whether or not he should present himself to Schumann. He left Mehlem with the intention of going to Düsseldorf, but he stopped at Cologne, on the suggestion of Wasielevsky, who had given him an introduction to Carl Reinecke. The famous pianist, at that time professor of piano and counterpoint at the Cologne Konservatorium, received Johannes and listened to his compositions, evidently with approval, for he took him to call on Ferdinand Hiller, the principal of the Konservatorium. Later, he escorted Johannes eastwards across the Rhine to Deutz and saw him into the train for Düsseldorf.

A FATEFUL MEETING

It was at the very end of September that Johannes first went to see the Schumanns. Joachim had paid them a visit a month earlier for the purpose of telling them about his new, wonderfully gifted young composer friend, and to prepare them for a possible call from him. The Schumanns' interest had thus been strongly aroused and when Johannes arrived he was given a warm welcome. Robert Schumann straightaway asked him to play his compositions, and at the end of the first movement of the sonata in C hurriedly fetched his wife

15

Clara to share in the exciting experience of hearing such convincing and original works so finely played. The two listened entranced to the remaining movements and begged for more and more. By the end of the longish programme a bond of mutual artistic and personal sympathy had been forged between the two Schumanns and Johannes. For him, the meeting marked the beginning of a new musical life. He stayed on in Düsseldorf for a month, frequently visiting his two new friends. As his knowledge of Robert Schumann deepened, the more he admired and venerated him; he also developed an adoration for the beautiful and richly gifted Clara. He discussed his own compositions with Schumann who advised him as to which he thought might be submitted for publication. When this was decided upon, Schumman wrote to Dr Härtel, of the Leipzig publishing firm Breitkopf & Härtel, asking if he would give favourable consideration to Johannes' compositions when he delivered the manuscripts to him. Johannes began the work of revising them.

Meanwhile, he had renewed his acquaintance with the Hamburg pianist Louise Japha, who had been the first to recommend Schumann's works to him a few months earlier, and who had latterly been living in Düsseldorf as a pupil of Clara Schumann's. He also met other members of the Schumanns' circle, with one of whom, Albert Dietrich, he formed a lasting friendship. The two met daily for talks over breakfast, and through Dietrich, Johannes was drawn into the company of painters as well as musicians—a circumstance that awakened in him an interest in the graphic arts which he never lost. With Dietrich he was closely associated in the composition of a sonata for violin and piano, which Schumann suggested should be written as a surprise for Joachim on his next visit to Düsseldorf towards the end of the month. Dietrich wrote the opening movement, Johannes, the scherzo, and Schumann, the intermezzo and finale. Joachim was not allowed to know beforehand which of the three had written the respective movements, but on performing the sonata at the party given by the Schumanns in his honour, he easily recognised the composers' individual musical styles.

After this festive occasion Joachim returned almost immediately to Hanover where he was joined at the beginning of November by Johannes. Shortly after his arrival there, and while he was still engaged in the preparation of his manuscripts for Breitkopf & Härtel, Johannes read, to his utter astonishment, the article Schumann had recently written about him in the *Neue Zeitschrift für Musik* (the journal which Schumann had edited ten years previously). In this long article 'New paths', published on October 28 1853, Schumann hailed Brahms as by far the greatest of all the new talents he had watched emerge in recent years. Describing him as 'one of the elect', he launched into a sustained eulogy of his personality and achievement. The article created a great stir in the musical world of the time, arousing both scepticism and opposition and awakening expectations which could not possibly be fulfilled for many years to come. Its main effect upon the innately modest Johannes, after he had recovered from the first shock of joyful surprise, was to sharpen his already strong faculty of self criticism. When he wrote to Schumann about a fortnight later to thank him for the encouraging opinion of his work expressed in the article, he told him that he had decided to weed out some of the compositions that had already been chosen for sending to Breitkopf: 'You will think it natural that I should wish to try with all my might to disgrace you as little as possible'. On mature thought he decided upon submitting only four works, numbering the piano sonata in C as op 1, the sonata in F sharp minor as op 2 (although it was written earlier than op 1), a group of six songs as op 3, and the scherzo in E flat minor as op 4. Breitkopf & Härtel accepted all the items and put their printing in hand at once. Of the fees paid to Johannes for these compositions he characteristically sent the greater part home to his parents as a gift.

FIRST VISIT TO LEIPZIG

Schumann had all along been anxious for Johannes to go to Leipzig to introduce his compositions to Dr Härtel by playing them himself, but Johannes had conducted the transaction by post from Hanover. However, once the matter was settled, he felt he ought to pay a visit to his new publisher. He arrived in Leipzig on November 17 and had the good fortune to be sought out the very next morning by a young 'Schumannite', Heinrich von Sahr, then living in the city. He installed Johannes in his own rooms as his guest and introduced

17

him to a number of Leipzig musicians, among whom were Felix Moscheles, the pianist and composer, the conductor Julius Rietz, Ferdinand David, leader of the famous Gewandhaus orchestra, and Julius Otto Grimm, then a student at the Leipzig Konservatorium and soon to become an intimate friend of Johannes for the remainder of his life.

Schumann's article championing Johannes had already brought his name into prominence in Leipzig, one of the principal musical centres of Germany, and his presence there now created considerable interest. He had probably counted on being allowed to play his compositions to Dr Härtel, but he could hardly have expected that within the space of a few days he should be playing his violin sonata with the redoubtable Ferdinand David; that another Leipzig publishing firm, Bartholf Senff, should express a wish to see any compositions he might like to send them; or that he should be persuaded to accept an engagement to perform as solo pianist at a Gewandhaus chamber concert later in the season.

At the end of a propitious week Johannes returned to Hanover to discuss with Joachim which compositions he should offer to Senff and who should be the dedicatees of the four works then being printed by Breitkopf. Between them they decided that op 1 should be inscribed to Joachim, op 2 to Clara Schumann and op 4 to Schumann's friend Ernst Wenzel. The songs op 3 were dedicated to Bettina (Brentano) von Arnim, of literary renown, who with her daughter Gisela had been present at the Schumanns' party when the sonata composed for Joachim had been performed. They were friends of his, whom Johannes came to know more intimately in Hanover.

To Senff, Johannes sent his sonata for violin and piano in A op 5, and a second set of six songs op 6; but the sonata was returned, as Senff did not publish works for violin. In its place Johannes sent his piano sonata in F minor, now finally completed. It was published as op 5 and dedicated to a friend of Grimm's, the Countess Ida von Hohenthal, in gratitude for her appointing, at Johannes' suggestion, his brother Fritz as music teacher to her children. The songs op 6 were dedicated to Louise Japha and her sister Minna. The

18

manuscript of the rejected violin sonata was unaccountably lost a few weeks later, and only the violin part has ever been recovered.

Johannes was back in Leipzig in time to attend a festival event on December 1—a concert which included works by Berlioz. The composer had come from Paris to conduct them, and Liszt came from Weimar with some of his followers to support him. Feeling was running high between the Leipzig ' academics '—some of whom were adherents of Mendelssohn and others, of Schumann—and the ' New German ' revolutionaries headed by Liszt and Wagner; but Johannes managed to steer a safe passage between the opposing factions. Opinions of his music were certainly divided, but his unassuming bearing and striking appearance won many hearts. He showed hs impartiality by going to call on Liszt at his hotel; a visit which Liszt referred to not long afterwards in a letter he wrote from Weimar to Hans von Bülow: '. . . Brahms, in whom I am sincerely interested and who behaved towards me tactfully and with good taste when I was in Leipzig '. And as for Berlioz, he enthusiastically embraced Johannes after hearing him play his sonata in C and scherzo in E flat minor at a crowded reception given on December 4 by Franz Brendel, then editor of the *Neue Zeitschrift für Musik*.

Johannes stayed on in Leipzig to perform these same two compositions at a David Quartet concert, between a Mendelssohn quartet and a Mozart quintet at the Gewandhaus on December 17. He received some sympathetic notices in the Leipzig press. In the *Signale* he was characterised as ' one of those highly gifted natures, an artist by the grace of God . . . He will, advancing steadfastly and safely along his "new paths", someday become what Schumann has predicted of him, an epoch making figure in the history of art.'

The momentous journey was coming to an end. Johannes returned to Hamburg on December 20, to his parents' infinite joy. They could well exult in his homecoming, for during the seven months of his absence he had achieved far more than they could ever have dared to hope for him. The name of Brahms had become known in musical centres across the length and breadth of Germany; the young composer had secured publishers for his works and he had entered into the first of many intimate friendships with key figures —with Joachim, the two Schumanns, Albert Dietrich and Julius

Grimm—which he was to form and maintain all through his career.

Brahms did not allow himself more than a few days respite in Hamburg. He paid calls on his former teachers Cossel and Marxsen, gave or sent copies of his printed compositions to friends as Christmas presents, visited some of his old haunts, and left for Hanover during the first week of January 1854.

STRESS AND TENSION

The new year seemed full of promise. Brahms took lodgings of his own in Hanover, began to compose his trio in B and spent as much as possible of his free time with Joachim and with his new Leipzig friend Julius Grimm, who had now settled in Hanover. At this time Brahms met and became friends with Hans von Bülow, a Liszt pupil, an adherent of the ' New German ' school and later a famous conductor. He was the first pianist, apart from the composer himself, to perform a Brahms work in public—the opening movement of the C major sonata, at Hamburg during the spring of that year (1854).

Towards the end of January Schumann came from Düsseldorf with his wife to spend a week in Hanover to hear performances of his own works, Joachim conducted his fourth symphony and Beethoven's piano concerto in E flat with Clara as soloist, and he also played a fantasy for violin and orchestra which Schumann had written especially for him the year before.

In less than a month after this happy reunion with their friends, Brahms and Joachim were appalled to read in a Cologne newspaper that Schumann had become mentally deranged, had thrown himself into the Rhine, had been rescued from drowning and taken back to his home, demented. Joachim wrote at once to Dietrich for confirmation of the news, but Brahms, agonised for his revered champion, did not even wait for a reply. He rushed off immediately to Düsseldorf to lend all the support he possibly could to Clara, thus tragically deprived of her adored husband and breadwinner, with six young children to care for and another expected. Her doctor thought it inadvisable that she should see her husband in his distraught condition. He was sent by his own wish to a private asylum at Endenich near Bonn.

During the next few months Brahms and Dietrich and others of Schumann's disciples did all they could to ease Clara's burden. Joachim came on short visits when his court duties at Hanover permitted; Grimm joined Brahms, who took over some of her teaching and helped to looked after the children, who became much attached to him. His attitude to Clara was one of filial devotion.

As the news from Endenich grew more hopeful, Clara took heart to listen to her husband's music played to her by the devoted young friends, and sometimes joined in the performances herself. In June her seventh child was born—a son, who was named Felix in remembrance of Mendelssohn and to whom Brahms was godfather. During her convalescence Brahms composed and dedicated to her his variations for piano op 9 on a theme by Schumann (the Album-blatt in F sharp minor op 99 no 4), upon which Clara had also composed variations (op 20) a year earlier. At Brahms's suggestion these two works were published simultaneously by Breitkopf in November, and at the same time, they brought out his trio in B op 8 and his third group of six songs op 7, dedicated to Dietrich. Only one other of his works was printed this year: the song 'Mondnacht', which appeared without opus number in a collection of songs by seven other composers published by a little-known firm in Göttingen. He also composed this year (1854) the four ballades for piano op 10, which he dedicated to Grimm but did not publish until 1856. The first of these pieces, which is based on the old Scottish ballad 'Edward', came into being as the result of another friendship Brahms made this year—with Julius Allgeyer, who was studying copperplate engraving in Düsseldorf. He introduced Brahms to Herder's *Stimmen der Völker* in which this ballad is included, as is also the 'Scottish lullaby' which inspired Brahms many years later to the composition of his well known intermezzo in E flat op 117 no 1.

During the earlier part of 1854 Brahms made his first attempts to write a symphony, in an effort to fulfil Schumann's expectations of him. He was helped by Grimm with the instrumentation, but he was not yet sufficiently well equipped to write a large-scale orchestral work. Rather than waste the three movements which he had completed, he transformed them into a sonata for two pianos. Later, he adopted two of these movements as the first and second of his piano concerto in D minor, and later still, he used the third as the second section ('Behold, all flesh is as grass') of the *German requiem*.

As soon as Clara Schumann was ready to begin life anew she decided to resume the career of travelling concert pianist which she had more or less relinquished on her marriage. Only thus could she hope to earn enough to support her family. In the autumn of 1854 she gave a series of concerts in north Germany with Joachim, playing several of Brahms's compositions among her solo items. As both Dietrich and Grimm had left Düsseldorf during the year to take up posts, it fell to Brahms to attend to Clara's business during her abence, and to act as messenger between Endenich and Düsseldorf. Schumann's condition varied from week to week, phases of lucidity alternating with relapses. The doctors would not allow Clara to seem him during the whole of his long illness, lest the excitement of a visit from her should prove disastrous to his mental balance. And so Brahms went from time to time to try to cheer him and to take news and messages to and from the pathetically divided couple. Joachim, too, periodically visited the afflicted man.

Towards the end of her north German tour Clara Schumann stayed a few days in Hamburg, and Brahms accordingly journeyed thither so that he might introduce her to his parents. It was very nearly a year since he had seen them and they were doubtless hoping he would stay over Christmas with them. But no, he felt he must devote himself entirely to Clara, and both he and Joachim accompanied her back to Düsseldorf to spend Christmas with her and her children.

CRISIS

Brahms published nothing in 1855, or indeed during the next few years, for he felt he now needed further study. With a view to strengthening his technique of composition he suggested to Joachim, of whose gift as a composer he held a high opinion, that they might both benefit by regularly exchanging exercises in counterpoint for mutual criticism. The exchanges should take place fortnightly, and if either of them failed to supply an exercise he should pay the other a fine to be spent on books or music. The two kept up this stimulating practice for several years.

But although Brahms was not composing large-scale works at this period (though he was making preliminary sketches for some), the year was musically eventful for him in other directions. His trio in B op 8 was given its first performance, not in Germany, but surprisingly, in New York, the pianist being William Mason, a member of an American musical family and a pupil of Liszt's. He had been present at the Altenburg when Brahms paid his first visit to Weimar in 1853. The trio was played again a few weeks later; this time in Breslau.

Brahms had now realised that as he could not hope to earn a sufficient income as a composer and teacher, he must try to augment his resources as a concert pianist. This year he played as soloist in Danzig in conjunction with a tour undertaken by Joachim and Clara, and performed for the first time with an orchestra in Beethoven's G major piano concerto at Bremen. He also played the 'Emperor' concerto in Hamburg late in the year, after which he returned yet again to Düsseldorf to spend Christmas 1855 with Clara.

By now, Clara knew that Schumann's recovery was beyond hope and she had so reorganised her domestic and professional life that she no longer needed Brahms's constant attention. He returned to Hamburg early in 1856, played Mozart's D minor piano concerto there during the celebrations for the centenary of Mozart's birth, undertook other concert engagements in Leipzig, Kiel and Altona and stayed with his parents until the end of March.

Early in April, when Clara Schumann left Düsseldorf for a long concert tour in Great Britain, Brahms took up residence in Bonn to be as near as possible to Schumann in case of a sudden emergency. Staying in Bonn gave him the opportunity of renewing contact with his friend Dietrich, who held a conductor's post there; and there, too, at the annual musical festival, he first met the great singer Julius Stockhausen, with whom he formed another of his close friendships. The two were soon giving concerts together in Bonn and Cologne.

And now Schumann's life was ending. Clara returned home at the end of her tour and was summoned by telegram to Endenich in time to see her husband two days before his death on July 29. After the funeral had taken place Brahms and Joachim accompanied her home to Düsseldorf and remained there for a time to support her in her grief and exhaustion, and also, at her request, to put Schumann's papers in order. Brahms again took over some of Clara's teaching engagements, and during the late summer escorted her on a much-needed holiday, to the Lake of Lucerne, with some of her children and his own sister Elise as companion. In the autumn Clara was ready to resume concert work and Brahms returned to Hamburg.

Brahms's utter devotion to Clara had originated in his gratitude and his sense of responsibility to Schumann who had so generously launched him upon his career, but it had subsequently developed from a different source. After sharing Clara's daily life for many months and experiencing countless opportunities for admiring her courage and the extreme nobility of her character, he had fallen deeply in love with this beautiful woman and incomparable pianist who was fourteen years older than himself. Even as early as in December 1854 he had written to her that he was ' dying of love for you ', and this emotional tension continued until after Schumann's death. To what extent Clara reciprocated Brahms's love can never be known, for all her letters to him during this period, and most of his to her, are no longer in existence. Only a few entries in her diary bear witness to the very warm affection she felt for her youthful admirer. When Clara was widowed and Brahms might possibly have asked her to share his life, he broke away abruptly and rededicated himself to his career as a composer—the only career that really mattered to this egotistical though generous-hearted young musician of twenty three. Clara remained what she had long been—a high priestess of her art and a loving, solicitous mother of her children.

That both she and Brahms suffered at the time of this sudden parting of their ways was inevitable, but the strength of their mutual attachment can be gauged from the fact that they remained devoted friends all their lives. It was perhaps only to be expected that two such supremely individual characters should come into conflict from time to time. Brahms was moody, and when he was in a bad frame of mind could all too easily offend Clara's finer sensibilities. She was deficient in a sense of humour and was inclined to treat Brahms's playfully intended taunts with deadly seriousness. She could also irritate him by her vagueness over matters of musical importance. Nevertheless, they remained fundamentally indispensable to each other's happiness. As time went on Brahms invariably sought Clara's opinion and advice on his compositions before he published them; he looked after her and her children whenever they needed his care and he was brokenhearted at her death in 1896, only a year before his own. Admittedly he fell in and out of love with younger women from time to time, but none of them ever usurped Clara's place in his heart of hearts.

A FIRST APPOINTMENT

Once back in Hamburg in 1857 Brahms busied himself with composition and teaching, but lived in a state of indecision about his immediate future. A partial solution presented itself from an unexpected quarter.

Among the pupils whom he had taken over from Clara Schumann in Düsseldorf the previous year was a Fräulein von Meysenbug, whose brother was connected with the princely court of Lippe Detmold. Brahms had made such a good impression upon her and her family while they were staying in Düsseldorf that they suggested he should pay a visit to them at Detmold. In the spring he accepted an invitation to spend a few days with them there, when he was asked to the castle to join in the court music-making by playing a Beethoven concerto and some solos, and by taking part in Schubert's 'Trout' quintet. His fine musicianship was so keenly appreciated by the court authorities that he was thereupon engaged to spend the three autumn months at Detmold, with the duties of giving piano lessons to the princess, playing at the court and conducting an amateur choral society of which the princely family were members. This appointment not only guaranteed Brahms some measure of financial security and left him free for nine months in the year, but it also gave him wider experience of handling musical forces. Admittedly, he found rigid court etiquette irksome, but he revelled in the surrounding woodland scenery and enjoyed the gay company of the youthful Charles von Meysenbug, his former pupil's nephew.

He held this appointment for three successive seasons and was much liked at the court, despite his native gaucherie. Between spells of duty he made his headquarters at Hamburg, engaging in other, socially less exacting forms of activity, musical and recreational. During the three year period in question he composed a steady succession of works, some of them in media new to him. They included the piano concerto in D minor, the first set of Hungarian dances for piano, some short pieces for organ, an *Ave Maria* for women's voices with orchestra (or organ), and the two orchestral serenades. He spent part of his summer holiday in 1858 in Göttingen with Grimm, who was now married and held a conductor's post in the small university town. Clara Schumann was there, too, with some of her children, for whom Brahms now wrote the ' *Children's folksongs,* with added accompaniments, dedicated to the children of Robert and Clara Schumann ', which was published anonymously at the end of the year.

At Göttingen that summer Brahms was strongly attracted by the daughter of one of the professors, Agathe von Siebold, who possessed a beautiful singing voice and who inspired the composition of two more sets of songs, op 14 and op 19. He was back in Göttingen again at the beginning of 1859, when he paid more noticeable attention to Agathe, and even went so far as to exchange engagement rings with her in secret. After he had left Göttingen the little town was fully expecting to hear the announcement of their betrothal, and Grimm, hoping to spare Agathe the embarrassment of current gossip, wrote to Brahms telling him he must declare his intentions. Once again, Brahms drew back, in apprehension at the very thought of marriage. With sublime indifference to Agathe's feelings he wrote to her saying that he loved her but that ' he could not wear fetters ', and asking if he might come back to Göttingen to see her. In replying, Agathe released him from the engagement, but she did so with a breaking heart and bore the wound for many years until she eventually married. Brahms's callous behaviour led to an estrangement between the Grimms and himself, which was fortunately not of long duration. He realised only too keenly how badly he had treated Agathe and in future was more circumspect in his relations with women. An inveterate bachelor, he carried on mild flirtations down the years but was careful never to break another heart.

Apart from this unhappy incident, the year 1859 was one of progress for Brahms as composer, performer and conductor. He was invited to play his piano concerto in D minor three times in fairly close succession—in January under Joachim in Hanover and under Rietz in Leipzig, and again under Joachim in March. Audiences at all three performances were perplexed by this explosive music, and in reactionary Leipzig the reception of the work was devastatingly hostile. At the Hamburg Philharmonic concert on March 24, however, the first appearance in the city of the splendid singer Julius Stockhausen, and the participation of Joachim both as soloist and conductor, combined to create an atmosphere favourable to the nervous young pianist and to secure him an enthusiastic welcome. Four days later the three musicians gave a concert together at which Brahms acted as accompanist to his two fellow artists. His serenade no 1 in D op 11, in its original form as an ' octet for strings and wind instruments ', received a successful first performance.

It was not long before Brahms found himself unexpectedly holding an appointment in Hamburg in addition to the one at Detmold, whither he was due to return in September. One of his favourite piano pupils, Friedchen Wagner, was also a keen choral singer and used to gather a few friends to join her at home in performing some of Brahms's choral compositions and arrangements under his own direction. It happened that in May that year (1859), Brahms played the organ at a wedding at the church of St Michael, accompanying a motet for women's voices which was composed by his friend Carl Grädener and sung by the pupils of his vocal school. Brahms was so delighted with the sound of the fresh young voices in the large building that he yearned to hear a performance under similar conditions of his own *Ave Maria,* which had already been given at Detmold. Friedchen collected the requisite number of voices, and after several rehearsals of the *Ave Maria* at her home and a performance in the church, the band of singers

27

formed themselves into a permanent choir to practise weekly under Brahms's direction. Their number was soon increased to forty and thus Brahms became the conductor of the 'Hamburg Ladies' Choir', an honorary post of great value to him in providing a stimulus to the composition of the long series of small-scale choral pieces, sacred and secular, which forms a good-sized section of his total work.

SETBACK AND RECOVERY

Having become disillusioned with the limitations of the music-making at Detmold Brahms resigned his post at the end of his third season there. From the beginning of 1860 he was more or less anchored to Hamburg by his ladies' choir. At the back of his mind, too, was the thought that he might perhaps be chosen to succeed the now elderly conductor of the Hamburg Philharmonic Orchestra who was due for retirement in the near future. In February Brahms conducted the first performance of his second serenade, and in March the final, orchestral version of the first serenade was given by royal command at Hanover under Joachim. All the same, Brahms was far from satisfied with his prospects, and for some time past he had been constantly irritated by the propaganda of the 'New German' school, whose members seemed to take it for granted that all contemporary German musicians were in sympathy with their aims, which to him were anathema. Unable to restrain his indignation any longer he persuaded Joachim to join him in writing a 'manifesto' against the aims of the 'New Germans'. It was intended for endorsement by a number of prominent, like-minded musicians, but while it was being circulated for signatures it inexplicably reached the offices of the Berlin journal *Echo,* and was printed prematurely with only four signatures: those of Brahms, Joachim, Grimm and Bernhard Scholz (then conductor of the Hanover Court Theatre). Needless to say, the inadequately sponsored document called forth scorn and ridicule from the opposing party. Brahms learned once and for all the wisdom of keeping his own counsel, and despite the obloquy heaped upon him in later years, by Wagner, Hugo Wolf and others, he stead-fastly declined to wield his pen publicly in self-defence.

The ignominious failure of the manifesto was counterbalanced by a series of successful happenings over the next few years, when Brahms was all the time quietly consolidating his position as a composer. A stroke of good fortune befell him in the summer of 1860 when he was attending the Rhine musical festival at Bonn. He met the man who was to become his principal publisher and, in addition, his friend, adviser and trustee in business affairs—Fritz Simrock, then junior partner in the old established firm of N Simrock, of Bonn and Berlin. Simrock straightway inaugurated the new connection with Brahms by bringing out the second serenade op 16 (a month before Breitkopf published the first serenade op 11), the sextet in B flat op 18 and the four songs for women's voices, horn and harp op 17. From now on, Brahms could count upon seeing his works printed by one or other of his several publishers. Among these was the Swiss firm Rieter-Biedermann of Winterthur, who in 1861 issued the piano concerto in D minor op 15, the *Begräbnisgesang* (' Funeral hymn ') for choir and wind instruments op 13, the *Ave Maria* op 12, and the eight songs and romances op 14.

When Brahms resumed rehearsals with his choir in July 1860, one of the members whom he specially liked, Bertha Porubszky, a visitor from Vienna, had already returned to her native city, but not without having extolled its many delights to Brahms and strengthened his long cherished hope of journeying thither. All through 1861 and the first half of 1862 he was busily engaged, both in concert-giving—sometimes jointly with Joachim, Stockhausen and Clara Schumann—and in composing three large scale works: the two piano quartets in G minor op 25, and in A major op 26, and the ' Handel ' variations and fugue for piano op 24, as well as the first four numbers of the *Magelonelieder*.

During this period, Brahms's friend Dietrich, now court conductor at Oldenburg, came to visit Brahms, who presented him with the manuscript of the ' Handel ' variations. He in turn invited Brahms to perform the variations in Oldenburg and himself conducted a performance of the first serenade. Only a short time before this, the second serenade had been played in New York. Brahms's fame at home and abroad seemed to be growing, but a cruel disappointment awaited him at home. In the spring of 1862 the coveted post of conductor of the Hamburg Philharmonic Orchestra went to Stockhausen!

Brahms did not allow this untoward circumstance to spoil his friendship with Stockhausen—his partner as a lieder singer—but he became embittered at being, as he thought, publicly slighted in his own city. He had an intense affection for Hamburg and had longed to settle there permanently. Now, in September 1862, having already given up his ladies' choir, he took the first step towards finding a new centre of activity.

FIRST VISIT TO VIENNA

When he set out for Vienna, Brahms intended staying there only a few weeks, but in the event, he remained throughout the whole winter season. He fell in love with the beautiful city and its delightful parks, and from the very first felt happy among the easy-going Viennese whom he found immensely more open hearted than the reserved north Germans. Vienna welcomed him as warmly as had Leipzig a few years earlier. He discovered old friends from Hamburg—the composer Grädener and the former member of his ladies' choir Bertha Porubszky, who was shortly to marry Arthur Faber, who became one of the new friends Brahms made with his usual zest. Among them were the pianist Carl Tausig, a pupil of Liszt's, the famous music critic Eduard Hanslick, to whom Brahms later dedicated his waltzes op 39, and Gustav Nottebohm, the well known Beethoven scholar.

Brahms's first call was upon Julius Epstein, piano professor at the Vienna Konservatorium, who already knew some of his published works and who immediately arranged for a private performance of his two piano quartets by the members of the Hellmesberger Quartet. Josef Hellmesberger, who was the director of the Konservatorium, also included the G minor quartet, with Brahms at the piano, in one of his regular concerts in November. A few days later Brahms gave a concert of his own, at which he produced the A major quartet and played his 'Handel' variations and works by Bach and Schumann. His two serenades were performed on separate occasions during his sojourn in Vienna and he appeared successfully

30

at concerts several times, either as composer, or as solo pianist in classical music, or as accompanist in his own songs.

Among musicians whose acquaintance he made, the most distinguished was Wagner, who was staying near Vienna preparing to give concert performances of excerpts from his operas. Brahms undertook some copying of the orchestral parts of *Die Meistersinger* for him on the recommendation of Tausig, and on one occasion played his 'Handel' variations to Wagner, who was considerably impressed by them. The two men never became friends, although Brahms greatly admired Wagner as a composer and habitually defended his compositions against their detractors.

Brahms acquired a new publisher in Carl Anton Spina, who brought out two of his small choral works. Spina also presented him with the whole of Schubert's printed compositions and allowed him to study all the Schubert manuscripts then in his possession, and even to make copies of a few of them.

This first visit of Brahms to Vienna was decisive for his future plans. He did not take up residence there until some six years later, but he paid long or short visits to the city from time to time, gradually extending his musical contacts and his friendships with Viennese residents. The list of his compositions was growing apace: it had recently included the piano quintet in F minor op 34, the two sets of 'Paganini' variations for piano op 35, the second string sextet op 36, the first sonata for cello and piano op 38 (dedicated to a new Viennese friend, the cellist Josef Gänsbacher), the horn trio op 40 and the nine songs of op 32.

On leaving Vienna in the spring of 1863 Brahms travelled to Hamburg by way of Hanover to see Joachim, who had recently become engaged to an opera singer, Amalie Weiss. She was soon to be the dedicatee of Brahms's four duets for contralto and baritone op 28, and much later, a notable interpreter of his *Alto rhapsody* op 53. Back in Hamburg in time for his thirtieth birthday, he was dismayed to find that friction had developed between his parents. His elderly mother had become an invalid and his much younger father, now a member of the Hamburg Philharmonic Orchestra, was chaffing under the restrictions placed upon his

31

instrumental practice at home. Brahms's thoughtful efforts to restore domestic harmony were largely ineffective.

Just when he was planning to reassemble his ladies' choir Brahms received an invitation from Vienna to become conductor of the choral society known as the 'Singakademie'. He accepted, not without hesitation, and returned to Vienna in August to prepare and rehearse the society's programmes for the season. The first three concerts met with varying degrees of approval, some of the *a cappella* items which Brahms had chosen being considered unduly austere. The fourth, a request programme of Brahms's own works, was an undisputed success, and after a final concert in May 1864 he was elected conductor for the next three years. On second thoughts, however, he resigned the position in order to be relieved of the time-consuming administrative duties and to regain freedom for composing.

Among his piano pupils this winter had been the gifted and beautiful Elisabeth von Stockhausen. Brahms found himself in danger of falling seriously in love with her and so he discontinued the lessons. When, before long, she married the composer Heinrich von Herzogenberg, Brahms felt he could safely renew contact with her. A rare and enduring musical friendship developed between both the Herzogenbergs and himself. When they left Vienna for Leipzig in 1872 they kept up an intimate correspondence with Brahms over many years. It now forms one of the most delightful sections of the large collection of Brahms's letters. Elisabeth von Herzogenberg exerted a wholly benign influence upon Brahms, second only, perhaps, to that of his ever beloved Clara Schumann. To Elisabeth he later dedicated the two rhapsodies for piano op 79.

The summer of 1864 saw Brahms again in Hamburg, where he found that relations between his parents had worsened to a degree beyond their bearing. He felt bound to make arrangements for his mother and sister to live apart from his father, and he himself bore the brunt of the increased family expenditure, although his own resources were still far from ample. His brother Fritz did not volunteer any assistance.

After this sad quest Brahms visited Clara Schumann at her home in Lichtental (Baden) and found relaxation in the company of a group of international celebrities staying there, the singer Pauline Viardot-Garcia, Johann Strauss the 'waltz king', Ivan Turgenev, Anton Rubinstein and the German painter Anselm Feuerbach with his disciple Julius Allgeyer who was already a devoted friend of Brahms from Düsseldorf. His most important new friendship was with Hermann Levi, then conductor of the Karlsruhe opera and later famous as an interpreter of Wagner. Levi was to prove indefatigable in performing Brahms's compositions for many years to come.

In the autumn Brahms went back to Vienna for what turned out to be only a brief stay. In February 1865 he was called home to Hamburg to his dying mother, the victim of a stroke. Brahms was heartbroken at her death, which took place shortly before his arrival, and for long could find no inner peace. From the autumn of this year onwards he travelled restlessly on concert tours for months on end, during which he paid his first visit to Switzerland, where he found his piano music was becoming increasingly well known. He played his piano concerto in D minor successfully under Levi at Mannheim and attended a Brahms festival directed by Dietrich at Oldenburg in December 1866.

During this strenuous period a work of large proportions was taking shape in Brahms's mind, and eventually he needed a period of peace in which to concentrate upon its composition. The work was the *German requiem,* for which Brahms did not use the customary Latin text but made his own choice of passages from the scriptures in Luther's German. He began writing it while staying in Allgeyer's peaceful house in Karlsruhe in 1866, and completed it during the summer, which he spent in Switzerland, at Zürichberg, enjoying as ever friendships old and new—with Theodor Kirchner, a fellow 'Schumannite', the conductor Friedrich Hegar, and an amateur musician who was later to become one of his closest intimates and keenest supporters in Vienna, the distinguished German surgeon Theodor Billroth.

FAMILY AFFAIRS

When Brahms was in Vienna again during the winter of 1866 his father wrote to tell him that he had decided to remarry and that

33

2

he would like Johannes' opinion of his chosen partner. Brahms met, and entirely approved of, the bride to be, the twice widowed Frau Caroline Schnack, who was much younger than Jakob and had a son Fritz aged sixteen—nicknamed by Brahms 'the second Fritz'. The marriage, which took place in March 1867, proved ideal in every respect. Johannes had no further anxiety as to his father's happiness, and he himself cherished a lasting affection for his step-mother.

Early in 1867 Brahms and Joachim undertook a series of concerts in Austria and Hungary, which were financially so profitable that Brahms was able to invite his father to spend a holiday with him. From Vienna they went on tour in the Austrian alps which afforded immense pleasure to them both. Jakob had never before seen mountains; Johannes rejoiced in the old man's wonderment at them.

In December 1867 three sections of the requiem were performed in Vienna by the Gesellschaft der Musikfreunde (Society of Music Lovers) under their conductor Johann Herbeck at a Schubert memorial concert. Owing to under-rehearsal and to a misreading of the dynamic marking of the timpanist's long pedal point in the third section, the favourable impression created by the music as a whole was greatly impaired. The ideal performance was yet to come.

Brahms had sent a copy of the completed six sections of the requiem to his friend Dietrich at Oldenburg. He in turn had been responsible for passing on the score to Karl Reinthaler, municipal director of music at Bremen and organist of the cathedral. The happy outcome was that the work was put into rehearsal for per-formance in the cathedral on Good Friday (April 10 1868). Brahms travelled north to confer with Reinthaler, made his headquarters at Hamburg where he appeared once or twice as solo pianist, and then joined Stockhausen for a series of concerts in Berlin, Dresden, Kiel and Copenhagen. Stockhausen had meanwhile resigned the conductorship of the Hamburg Philharmonic, and once again Brahms was passed over—another reason, perhaps, for his pending decision to settle permanently in Vienna.

The coming performance of the requiem in Bremen cathedral aroused widespread interest and attracted distinguished musicians from many quarters, including England. On the occasion itself Brahms was nobly supported by the presence of many of his friends and of the two people dearest to him, his father and Clara Schumann. Stockhausen sang the baritone solo and the choral forces included four specially picked members of the Hamburg Ladies' Choir. The splendidly prepared performance, conducted by Brahms himself, was an unqualified success. With this, his first large scale choral orchestral work, Brahms achieved his greatest triumph so far. He proved beyond doubt that he had attained artistic maturity, and he was widely acclaimed as a master.

He wasted no time by basking in his new glory, but returned to Hamburg to prepare the score for publication (as op 45, by Rieter-Biedermann in 1868-69) and to compose the additional solo ' Ye now are sorrowful ' which became the fifth of the seven sections and thus completed the mighty whole. In this final version the requiem was performed all over Germany and in Switzerland the following year; in London in 1871 and 1873, St Petersburg and Utrecht in 1872 and Paris in 1875.

Far from being exhausted by the demands made upon him by the requiem, Brahms attended the Rhine festival at Cologne in June and there met and made friends with the composer Max Bruch. He retired to Bonn for the summer, not to rest, but to complete the cantata *Rinaldo* op 50, which he had begun in 1863 and which was his nearest approach to composing an opera. He also began to sketch the *Schicksalslied* (' Song of Destiny ') op 54. He took his father for a holiday in Switzerland and visited Clara Schumann at Oldenburg in October, where he gave with her the first (private) performance of the duet version of his Hungarian dances which were still in manuscript. After having joined Stockhausen for a few concerts in Germany during November he reached Vienna in time for Christmas. During this arduous year Brahms published five books of solo songs, op 43 and opp 46-49, twenty five songs in all, as well as two sets of partsongs, opp 42 and 44. He also completed the *Magelonelieder* op 33, which now comprised fifteen songs.

Brahms had no sooner taken up residence in Vienna in 1869 than he was offered two posts in Germany: Hiller invited him to become professor of piano at Cologne, Joachim wanted him to join the staff of the newly founded Berlin Hochschule für Musik to which he had been appointed director. Brahms declined both these offers, but when the possibility arose of his being invited to become director of the Vienna Gesellschaft der Musikfreunde in the not too distant future, he intimated that he might be willing to consider accepting.

He signalised his present contentment with Vienna by composing and publishing the graceful, carefree *Liebeslieder waltzer* for piano duet and four part chorus *ad lib* op 52. At their first performance, at Karlsruhe, the duettists were Clara Schumann and Hermann Levi. The work that immediately followed was entirely different in character and mood, and was the outcome of a personal sorrow.

Brahms had long been fond of Clara's beautiful third daughter Julie. While he was staying with the family at Lichtental during the summer of 1869 he fancied himself in love with her but gave no outward indication of his feelings. When Clara happened to mention to him that Julie had recently become engaged to an Italian count, he was taken by surprise and deeply wounded. He sought consolation in composing the dark toned *Alto rhapsody* for soloist, male chorus and orchestra op 53, with profoundly moving words taken from Goethe's *Harzreise im Winter*. He showed it, completed, to Clara soon after Julie's wedding in September and it became his first publication in 1870, the year of the Franco-Prussian war.

Although Brahms had chosen to live in Austria, he remained at heart a German patriot and was a great admirer of the chancellor Bismarck. He was so deeply stirred by the events of the war that at one time he thought seriously of volunteering as a soldier. He was too late. Victory was in sight and he diverted his military zeal into composing the *Triumphlied* for baritone solo, double choir and orchestra op 55. It was first performed in 1871, and so, too, was the *Song of destiny* op 54, which he had begun to write two years earlier. He published it this year, as well as two groups of solo songs, opp 57 and 58.

At the end of 1871 Brahms moved into the quarters which he was to occupy until the end of his life—a pair of rooms at no 4 Karls-gasse, close to the new building of the Gesellschaft der Musikfreunde. Early in January 1872 he was notified of his father's sudden grave illness. He hastened to Hamburg and remained at his father's side until he died a few days later, of cancer of the liver. Brahms stayed on in Hamburg to make provision for the future of his sister Elise and of his stepfamily, and from now onwards he contributed generously to their support. As he became more prosperous he increased the gifts of money he sent them regularly, and often paid for holidays which he suggested they should take. He established his stepbrother Fritz Schnack as a clockmaker in Holstein, and when Elise married a widower with six children, he undertook the education of the youngest boy. With Frau Caroline Brahms he maintained an affectionate correspondence until within a few days of his death.

THE BENEFICENT BRAHMS

It was not only to his family that Brahms was open handed; anyone in need could count on his support. Even beggars in the street never appealed to him in vain. The money he earned with his compositions and with fees for performing engagements eventually amounted to far more than he needed to satisfy his own simple tastes. He asked his publisher Fritz Simrock to administer the accumulated funds and to apply them as he thought best to help needy musicians. Brahms did not wish his name to be known to the beneficiaries; he preferred to do good by stealth. Not long before the end of his life he received a legacy of £1,000 from an English admirer whom he had never met, Adolf Behrens, who had already assumed financial responsibility for the first performance in England of Brahms's requiem, and also, much later, for engaging the Viennese clarinettist Richard Mühlfeld to take part in London performances of the Brahms clarinet trio and quintet. The composer, who was deeply touched by the kindly thought that prompted the legacy, immediately divided the money between various good causes including a gift of 6,000 Austrian florins to the Gesellschaft der Musikfreunde on condition that fl 1,000 be given to the museum, and that the strictest secrecy be kept as to the name of the donor. When Bülow's sixtieth birthday was celebrated by a gift to him from Hamburg friends of 10,000 German marks to be devoted to an artistic aim, Brahms showed great imagination in recommending an appropriate purpose. A zealous editor of early music himself, he suggested, and Bülow agreed, that the money might be presented as a complimentary gift to the great musical scholar Friedrich Chrysander, who had nearly completed his monumental edition of the complete works of Handel.

ARTISTIC DIRECTOR

On coming back from Hamburg to Vienna in 1872, Brahms decided to accept the proffered position of artistic adviser to the Gesellschaft der Musikfreunde. He was given wide powers and when he took up his duties in the autumn he made sweeping changes in the orchestral personnel and instituted more frequent choral practices. The concert programmes that he planned (six in every season), which included a high proportion of music from earlier periods, made heavy demands on performers and audiences alike, but Brahms's fine sense of historic style when he was conducting ensured interpretations that satisfied all concerned. He held this exacting but rewarding post for three years, and although his time for composition was inevitably curtailed, he produced a number of important works. In 1873 the most noteworthy were his first two string quartets op 51, the ' Haydn ' variations in two versions—for orchestra op 56A, and for two pianos op 56B—and eight songs op 59, which included the well known *Regenlied* and *Nachklang*. In 1874 came three collections of smallish choral pieces, op 61, 62 and 64, the nine solo songs of op 63 and the second set of *Liebeslieder Waltzer* op 65A; in 1875, the piano quartet in C minor op 60 (begun long before), and the third string quartet in B flat op 67. During the summer of 1874 Brahms attended a music festival at Zürich to conduct his *Triumphlied*. There he met the Swiss poet J V Widmann, with whom he formed a close friendship.

When Brahms resigned his post in 1875 he was elected an honorary member of the Gesellschaft der Musikfreunde. During that year he began to serve on the panel of a government commission on education which granted financial aid to gifted musicians. In his official capacity he was able to help Dvořák by recommending him for a grant, and he assisted him still further by

38

introducing him personally to his own publisher Simrock, who was so much interested in Dvořák's compositions that he commissioned him to write the *Slavonic dances* which were to bring a fortune to both composer and publisher. Dvořák was ever after grateful to Brahms for his encouragement at the outset of his career.

By the mid 1870's Brahms's compositions were becoming so well known in European musical centres that he was besieged by invitations to play or conduct them. If he had acceded to all these requests his creative work would have been completely disrupted. He was obliged to come to a decision to undertake only such engagements as seemed most pressing, and he liked to fit them annually into the first three months of the year. He often went on holiday in late spring or early autumn, and in summer took up residence in the country, either in Austria or abroad, to devote his time to composition. During the autumn in Vienna he completed such works as he had already begun and supervised their printing and publication. All the year around he kept in touch with his friends, and on his holidays was always accompanied by one or more of them. Whether he was at home or away, his usual daily routine consisted in rising at about 5 am to go for a walk, in working all the morning and in spending the remainder of the day in alternating spells of work and leisure. In the evenings he relaxed completely and met his friends.

Brahms lived very frugally, even when he became more prosperous. He made his own, very strong, early morning coffee and took his meals at humble eating houses. Almost the only luxuries he allowed himself (beyond large cigars) were the Italian holidays of his later years and the acquisition of books and musical autographs, of which he gradually built up fine collections and left them by will to the Gesellschaft der Musikfreunde. During his lifetime he handed over to the Library 300 manuscript copies of Domenico Scarlatti's sonatas, a treasure beyond price.

Brahms had an apparently inexhaustible capacity for work. In addition to his exertions as composer, conductor and performer, he found time for a variety of secondary musical tasks, for instance, transcribing his own larger works for piano solo or duet so that he could play them to friends before they were published or performed; writing technical studies for piano and accompaniments to folksongs; orchestrating some of Schubert's songs; composing cadenzas to Mozart and Beethoven piano concertos, and so on. He also spent much time in proof-reading, in revising his own compositions and in functioning as joint editor of the collected works of at least seven great composers, including François Couperin, Schubert and Chopin. And somehow, he made time to write innumerable letters.

TOWARDS THE ZENITH 1876-89

Brahms had for long postponed completing the symphony that he attempted to write at Schumann's suggestion before he was thirty. In 1876, after he had spent the summer on the Baltic island of Rügen with the singer George (later Sir George) Henschel, his eagerly awaited first symphony in C minor op 68, was ready for performance. It was given a hearing in November at Karlsruhe under Otto Dessoff, the former conductor of the court opera in Vienna. It did not at first meet with complete acceptance, but its reception at the time, and later, was sufficiently cordial to spur Brahms on to the composition of another work in the same category. Within the space of a year the second symphony in D op 73 came into being and was first performed in December 1877 under Hans Richter in Vienna. It achieved an immediate and resounding success and was soon heard in various parts of Germany, and in London and Cambridge. An outstanding performance in 1878 was the one Brahms was invited to conduct at a concert given as part of the celebrations of the fiftieth anniversary of the Hamburg Philharmonic Society. The orchestra was led by Joachim, who had already conducted the symphony in Düsseldorf, and several of Brahms's personal friends came from a distance to play among the first violins. As the composer mounted the rostrum to conduct, looking immensely impressive with his recently grown flowing beard, he was presented wth a laurel wreath to the accompaniment of an orchestral flourish. At the end of the performance he received an overwhelmingly enthusiastic ovation. Hamburg was at last making amends for earlier neglect of her famous son.

Now in his early forties. Brahms was rising to the very height of his powers. Within the next dozen years he was to compose one masterpiece after another: symphonies, overtures, concertos and chamber sonatas. He was to win triumphs in other countries and to have honours showered upon him. The manifold events of this peak period are fully documented by his principal biographers. Only some of the more significant achievements can be summarised here.

Brahms had made his first concert tour in Holland in 1876 and there found great enthusiasm for his work. He could have experienced a similarly enthusiastic reception if he had come to England to accept the honorary doctorate in music which Cambridge offered to confer upon him this year. He could not face the journey, and as the degree could not be conferred *in absentia,* he had to forgo the honour. Fortunately for him, there was no obligation to be present in London when the Philharmonic Society awarded him its coveted gold medal the following year.

Another compliment paid to him in 1877 was an invitation to become municipal director of music at Düsseldorf. He weighed the proposition carefully, but finally decided against it, for he could not tear himself away from Vienna. When, in 1878, he was offered the post of Kantor of the Thomasschule in Leipzig (the post made famous by Bach), he turned it down, chiefly because the musical climate of Leipzig was uncongenial to him.

For Brahms, a memorable event of 1878 was the first of several spring holidays in Italy. On this occasion he was accompanied by his knowledgeable friend Billroth who acted as guide, and by the Hungarian composer Karl Goldmark. Brahms looked forward to the journey and he revelled in the southern scene and the glories of Italian art and architecture. On returning home he spent the summer at the Carinthian village of Pörtschach, there to compose his violin concerto op 77. It was designed especially for Joachim, who gave the first performance, with Brahms conducting, at the Leipzig Gewandhaus on New Year's day 1879. This concert made a propitious beginning to the year that was to include the composition of the first sonata for violin and piano op 78, and the publication of the first two books (op 76) of the much later series of

41

capricci and intermezzi for piano; concert tours with Joachim in Hungary and Transylvania and the offer from Breslau of an honorary doctorate in philosophy. It was expected that Brahms should acknowledge the honour by composing an orchestral work. Ironically enough, he responded with his notoriously unacademic *Academic festival overture* op 80, based on German students' songs. It was written at his new summer resort Ischl (Upper Austria) in 1880 and performed at Breslau under his own baton amid scenes of enthusiasm in January 1881. Brahms also wrote a companion piece of similar dimensions but strongly contrasted in character, the *Tragic overture* op 81. Composed at the same date as op 80, it was first performed a fortnight earlier, in Vienna in December 1880.

FIRST VISIT TO MEININGEN

These two sizeable compositions were far surpassed in magnificence by the titanic work Brahms produced during the summer of 1881 at Pressbaum, near Vienna. This was the second piano concerto in B flat major op 83, which he dedicated to the teacher of his boyhood, Edward Marxsen, now seventy five years of age. Brahms's friend Hans von Bülow, who had recently become director of music at the ducal court of Saxe Meiningen, gave him the opportunity of rehearsing the work privately with his orchestra soon after it was composed. A very successful public performance took place at the end of October at a concert consisting entirely of Brahms's own compositions.

Brahms's connection with the Meiningen orchestra led to friendship with the reigning duke George II and his consort, and to many informal music makings at the castle, as well as to holidays at the duke's country estate, Altenstein—to say nothing of two decorations conferred upon him by this music loving nobleman. More important was it that the duke allowed Bülow to take the orchestra on tour, largely for the purpose of making Brahms's works better known.

During the six years that elapsed between the production of his second symphony in 1877 and the third in 1883 Brahms wrote, in addition to the two concertos, the two overtures and the piano pieces already mentioned, his second piano trio op 81, his first string quintet op 88 and the last two of his smaller choral orchestral works. These were *Nänie* (Schiller) op 82, written as a tribute to his recently deceased friend Anselm Feuerbach and dedicated to the painter's mother, and *Parzenlied* ('Song of the Fates') (Goethe) op 89, dedicated to the duke of Meiningen. These two pieces were both first performed in Switzerland, where Brahms particularly admired the style of choral singing.

This very fertile and apparently smoothly running phase of Brahms's career was not unclouded by personal troubles, which were caused very largely by his own difficult temperament. His was a complex character. The same man who could be almost preposterously generous with his purse and prompt to help friends and even strangers when they were in need, could also be maladroit and tortuous with his pen and acrimonious in conversation. He seemed to take a perverse delight in living up to his reputation for sarcasm. Even his closest friends did not escape his wounding shafts. His later years were punctuated by periods of estrangement, short, long or permanent, from Joachim, Clara Schumann, Hermann Levi, Hans von Bülow and others. Already in 1873 Brahms had fallen out with Joachim over the arranging of programmes for the Schumann festival at Bonn, and Levi had been the peacemaker. Seven years later Brahms quarrelled violently with Levi over his growing partisanship for Wagner, and lost him altogether from his circle of friends. At about the same time, when Joachim was bringing divorce proceedings against his wife, Brahms tactlessly, if gallantly, took her part openly. This was more than Joachim could forgive. It was several years before their intimate friendship was restored, although in the meantime he did not cease to perform or conduct Brahms's works.

Having spent several consecutive summers at Ischl, Brahms broke new ground by going to Wiesbaden in 1883, there to complete the third symphony in F major op 90. He was drawn to this Rhineland spa because it was the home of the young mezzo soprano Hermine Spies, whom he had met earlier that year when she had performed in his *Parzenlied* at Crefeld. She sang her way into his heart by her beautiful interpretations of his songs; he was entranced by her gaiety and her ready understanding of his particular brand of humour.

Hermine was sufficiently shrewd to recognise that although the fifty year old composer was in love with her, he had no intention of marrying. This summer they enjoyed a happy companionship which was renewed from time to time over the years, and Hermine became the inspiration of many of Brahms's later songs.

The third symphony was first performed in December 1883 under Hans Richter in Vienna, where it met with only modified enthusiasm owing to the antagonism between the Wagner-Bruckner faction and Brahms's own partisans. The composition of the work had, however, effected a partial reconciliation with Joachim, whom Brahms begged to conduct the symphony in Berlin. In that city it was received so warmly in January 1884 that three additional performances followed in the same month, all of them conducted by the composer himself. And at Meiningen, Bülow performed the symphony twice in one programme.

Early in 1884 Brahms was offered, but would not accept, the post of conductor of the Cologne orchestra. He was planning the fourth symphony, and after a spring holiday on Lake Como, took up his summer quarters at the Styrian village of Mürzzuschlag, where he was visited by several of his friends from Vienna and by Clara Schumann.

Besides sketching the fourth symphony, he published this year two sets of partsongs op 92 and op 93A, the two songs with accompaniment for piano and viola op 91, two books of solo songs, op 94 and op 95, and a six part glee, a drinking song, *Dank der Damen* (' To the ladies ') op 93B, dedicated to ' his friends at Crefeld '. It was his last work for unaccompanied choir.

The fourth symphony in E minor op 98 was completed at Mürzzuschlag the next summer (1885). Brahms conducted the first performance at Meiningen and thereafter went on tour with the orchestra as ' spare conductor ' (his own description). In this capacity he conducted the symphony himself at each of the nine cities they visited in Germany and Holland, and Bülow conducted all the other items. The triumphal progress was suddenly shattered by a piece of clumsiness on the part of Brahms. While absent for a short time from the orchestra he let himself be persuaded into conducting the symphony at Frankfurt with the local orchestra, thus anticipating the performance soon to be given there by the Meiningen orchestra, which Bülow had especially wanted to conduct himself. The loyal, hypersensitive Bülow was so bitterly hurt by Brahms's seeming mistrust in the orchestra and in himself personally that he resigned the conductorship forthwith. Brahms was only temporarily embarrassed at the result of his thoughtlessness and did not take the matter seriously. Not until Bülow came to Vienna more than a year later to give a piano recital did he gracefully make amends. He sought Bülow out and the friendship and mutual trust were fully reinstated. The fourth symphony had meanwhile made great headway under Joachim's baton. It became his favourite of the four symphonies and brought him gradually nearer the complete reconciliation with Brahms that was to follow within a year or two.

ON LAKE THUN, 1886-1888

Brahms spent the next three summers in Switzerland, at Hofstetten near Thun, where he was within easy reach of his poet friend J V Widmann, with whom he spent many weekends and from whom he borrowed countless books. At Hofstetten he was visited by the north German poet Klaus Groth, some of whose poems he had set to music and who shared his enthusiasm for Hermine Spies. She, too, came on occasional visits and made music with Brahms at the Widmanns' house to their mutual delight.

Despite these social distractions Brahms's inspiration flowed without interruption. During the three years he composed the second cello sonata op 99, the piano trio in C minor op 101, the double concerto for violin and cello op 102—the last of his orchestral works and a final, effective peace offering to Joachim in 1887—the violin sonatas in A major op 100 and in D minor op 108 (often known as the ' Thun sonatas '), the eleven *Zigeunerlieder* (' Gipsy songs ') op 103, three books of songs op 105-107, and five partsongs for unaccompanied mixed choir op 104. In the intervals he spent short spring holidays in Italy; with Simrock and Kirchner in 1887 and with Widmann the following years. With the latter he discussed at some length the possibility of their collaborating in the production of an opera. But although Widmann was ready to provide a

45

libretto, Brahms could not summon up courage to tackle a musical setting.

Just at this time Brahms had to face a domestic problem arising from the death of the last member of the family whose lodger he had been during the past many years in the Karlsgasse. He did not want to move, and so he took over the empty flat in addition to his own quarters, and needed someone who would keep all the rooms in order. One of the most perceptive of his Viennese friends, Frau Fellinger, solved the problem for him by finding an ideal tenant for the flat—Celestine Truxa, the widow of a journalist, who was willing to attend to all Brahms's personal and domestic needs. After she had come to live in the flat upstairs, bringing her two young sons with her, Brahms had no more household cares. Until his death he was most kindly looked after by the capable, unobtrusive Frau Truxa. The two little boys were an especial delight and interest to him. Brahms had always loved children and made friends with them wherever he went.

GROWING OLDER

Brahms was beginning to age. He reduced the number of his concert tours and did not go so far afield for his summer sojourns, which he now resumed at Ischl. Since his election as honorary president of the Vienna Tonkünstlerverein (Musicians' Society) he spent more time in the company of his fellow musicians. He made an especial friend of the society's new archivist Eusebius Mandyczewski, who took burdensome routine tasks off Brahms's hands, assisted him in his collecting of folksongs, and after his death, became the principal editor of his collected works.

While at Ischl in 1889 Brahms received two new honours—the Order of Leopold from the Austrian emperor, and the honorary freedom of the city of Hamburg, the latter a privilege granted to him through a suggestion of Bülow's to the burgomaster. As a token of gratitude to Hamburg Brahms composed the three *Fest- und Gedenksprüche* for unaccompanied choir op 109, which were performed in the city in September and dedicated to the burgomaster. To Bülow, who celebrated his sixtieth birthday a few months later, Brahms presented the autograph of his third symphony.

Four years later (1894) Hamburg paid Brahms another intended compliment by offering him the conductorship of the Philharmonic Orchestra which had already eluded him on two previous occasions. Now that he was too elderly to feel inclined to accept, he replied to the invitation with hardly disguised sarcasm: '. . . there is little that I have desired so long and so ardently in its time: that is to say, the right time . . .'. He went on to hope the committee would find a younger man who could work for them as devotedly as he himself would have done.

After his annual Italian holiday, with Widmann in the spring of 1890, Brahms composed his second string quintet op 111 at Ischl. He felt that it might well be his last work of any size and that he ought now to go through all his manuscripts, revising or destroying them in order to eliminate any he considered unworthy to survive. He prepared for publication the six vocal quartets op 112, which he had begun in 1888, and the collection of thirteen canons for women's voices op 113, originally composed for his Hamburg choir. He also drew up a very detailed will, which he subsequently remade on his sister's death in 1892. (His brother had died in 1886.) Unfortunately, he neglected to sign this new will; an omission that led to an infinity of legal complications after his death.

The year 1891 brought Brahms a revivifying experience. Listening in March to the Meiningen orchestra under its new conductor Fritz Steinbach, Brahms was profoundly impressed by the beautiful playing of the clarinettist Richard Mühlfeld. It inspired him to compose the clarinet trio op 114 and the clarinet quintet op 115, both of which were first performed in Berlin in December the same year at one of the Joachim Quartet concerts, with Mühlfeld playing the clarinet parts. In the audience was the septuagenarian German painter and engraver Adolf Menzel. He was moved to make a symbolical drawing of the performance as a gift to Brahms, with whom he enjoyed some festive meetings and lively discussions on art and music. They were both members of the Prussian order ' Pour la Mérite '.

The autumn of the same year was darkened for Brahms by the last and most serious of all his estrangements from intimate friends. In October his friendship with Clara Schumann came nearly to breaking point. Clara, who was now seventy two and worn down by persistent anxieties and ill health, had often been hurt by Brahms's growing embitterment, aloofness and seeming lack of cordiality towards herself. The immediate cause of the threatened rupture in 1891 was the publication of the original draft of Schumann's third symphony, which Clara had handed over to Brahms and which he considered preferable to the final, revised version. He had discussed the scheme with Clara and was under the impression that she was fully in agreement with it, but when she read in the *Signale* of the forthcoming publication of this draft as a ' Schumann relic ' under the editorship of Brahms's conductor friend Franz Wüllner, she was immediately up in arms, wrongly surmising that this was a money-making enterprise, and taxing Brahms with a breach of confidence. The hostile letter she wrote to him elicited a very temperate reply from Brahms, explaining that no question of money was involved, and that Wüllner was so much better equipped for the task than he himself. A second, peremptory letter from Clara seemed to Brahms to forbid further communication. For a few weeks he remained silent and withdrawn, but at Christmas he took a first step towards a reconciliation by sending Clara a letter of greeting which slightly eased the tension. A few letters passed between them, but only in September 1892, after Brahms had written Clara a birthday letter that was largely an appeal for the restitution of the friendship which meant so much to him, did Clara capitulate completely. Their letters now took on their customary tone of mutual sympathy and Clara signified her restored confidence by entrusting Brahms with the sole editing of a supplementary volume of the Schumann *Collected edition,* which was to contain some of the compositions that had previously been held back. After this near catastrophe, Brahms did everything in his power to surround Clara with all the love and tenderness she sorely needed during her few remaining years, and she in turn responded warmly.

THE PIANIST BRAHMS

Brahms had published nothing for piano solo since the first two books (op 76) of capricci and intermezzi and the two rhapsodies op 79 which he brought out in 1879-80. Now, during the years

1891-93, he completed four more books of single pieces, similar in type but musically of a deeper significance. These were the fantasias op 116, three intermezzi op 117, six pieces (including a ballade and a romance) op 118, and four pieces op 119, the last of which is the rhapsody in E flat. Brahms sent a copy of the elegiac intermezzo in E flat minor op 118 No 6 as a gift to Clara in May 1893, telling her that it was ' teeming with dissonances, exceptionally melancholy and could hardly be played too slowly '. Clara entered in her diary that the dissonances were of a kind ' to which one could surrender oneself ecstatically '.

In their concentrated expressiveness this whole group of pieces, op 116-119, formed a striking contrast to the virtuosic compositions of Brahms's younger days, such as the ' Handel ' and the ' Paganini ' variations, which made immense demands upon his then formidable performing technique. At the outset of his career it was often his playing rather than his compositions that won attention from the critics. How Brahms played when he was twenty one may be gathered from a letter of Joachim's written in 1854 to Gisela von Arnim: ' . . . he plays divinely. I have never heard piano playing (except perhaps Liszt's) which gave me so much satisfaction—so light and clear, so cold and indifferent to passion . . . I have never come across a talent like this before.'

Brahms's subtle art of interpretation both of his own and of other composers' work was evidently the distinguishing feature of his performances. His pupil and biographer Florence May wrote of it: ' Not the playing of a virtuoso, but expressing the very depth of whichever music he played.'

In due course, however, Brahms's preoccupation with composing led him to neglect his playing, which then gradually deteriorated in accuracy and finish. The singer Stockhausen made an illuminating comment in a letter to Clara Schumann in 1868: ' Brahms is prac-tising like mad today at the Schumann concerto, that is to say, he is learning it by heart; for as you know, there is seldom any question of real practising with him. He is certainly a great musician; such culture joined to such knowledge I have never met, but a piano player he will never be; any sort of practice bores him so that he just plays . . . Even the accompaniment of songs is too much trouble for him. . .' His playing evidently depended very much upon his mood of the moment. Eugenie Schumann wrote of hearing him in a ' wholly unenjoyable performance ' of her father's quartet in E flat, and Stockhausen once reported to his wife that ' Brahms accompanied the French air even worse than he did in Hamburg . . .' But according to one of his more recent biographers, Richard Specht, who heard him play towards the end of his life, Brahms then cultivated an intimate style of performance which was perfectly in keeping with the meditative character of some of his own last pieces. His techniques of performance and of composition had become reconciled on a new plane.

INDIAN SUMMER

In 1893 Brahms spent his sixtieth birthday quietly with Widmann in the south of Italy, where he had fled to escape being lionised during the many festive events which he knew were being devised to commemorate the event. In 1892 he had again declined the renewed offer of an honorary doctorate in music from Cambridge, but on his return to Vienna from Italy in 1893 he was awarded a distinction which he was delighted to accept. It was a gold medal bearing his portrait, struck in his honour by the Gesellschaft der Musikfreunde, who also gave him fifty replicas in bronze to distribute among his friends.

The next year (1894) he completed and published his collection of forty nine German folksongs for solo voice and piano, and composed the two sonatas for clarinet and piano op 120, again for Mühlfeld, whom he nicknamed his ' prima donna ' or ' Fräulein Klarinette '. The composing of the sonatas seemed to give Brahms a new lease of life, for he went on tour with Mühlfeld in 1895 to play them at concerts in Leipzig, Frankfurt, Rüdesheim and Meiningen. This year was musically the most eventful of his last period. In January, during a ' Brahms week ' in Leipzig, he conducted a concert when the brilliant young pianist Eugen d'Albert played both his concertos. He attended a three day festival in September in Meiningen devoted to works by the ' Three B's ' (Bach,

Beethoven and Brahms), at which several representative compositions of his own were performed under Fritz Steinbach. In October he went to Zürich to conduct his *Triumphlied* at the concert given to inaugurate the city's new concert hall, where he had the satisfaction of seeing his portrait on the painted ceiling side by side with those of Mozart and Beethoven. Before the end of the year he visited Clara at Frankfurt, where she played to him for the last time, and finally, he was awarded the Medal for Art and Science by the Austrian emperor.

Brahms needed these stimulating experiences, for his last few years were saddened by the deaths of several close friends in quick succession: Eduard Marxsen, Gustav Nottebohm, Elisabeth von Herzogenberg, Theodor Billroth and Hans von Bülow. Hermine Spies, too, had died in 1894 at the early age of thirty six, but even before her death, Brahms had come under the spell of yet another singer. Alice Barbi, a youngish Italian contralto resident in Vienna, was his last sweetheart, and the most sympathetic, in his opinion, of all the fine interpreters of his songs.

The worst loss of all was to follow in 1896. Clara Schumann was taken seriously ill in April and suffered a stroke. On hearing of this, Brahms gave up a projected journey to Meran and remained in Vienna awaiting news of her recovery or a summons to Frankfurt if her condition worsened. During this anxious period he composed *Vier ernste Gesänge* ('Four serious songs') for bass voice op 121. He completed them in time for his sixty third birthday, when he was overjoyed to receive a scribbled note of greeting from Clara. He replied at once to express his delight.

Not many days later the blow fell; a telegram reached Brahms informing him that Clara had died on May 20. He left Ischl immediately by train to attend the funeral at Frankfurt, but owing to a mischance en route he was travelling for forty hours. He arrived in Frankfurt too late for the service and reached Bonn, completely exhausted, only just in time for the interment. His anguish at losing Clara and the strain of the long journey prostrated him. After recovering from a severe chill he returned to Ischl. During the summer he composed the set of eleven chorale preludes for organ op 122, which proved to be his last work and were not published during his lifetime.

THE LAST PHASE

It was not long before a change began to take place in Brahms's appearance. The sturdily built, now rather corpulent composer, who had enjoyed robust health ever since his boyhood, was losing weight and the colour of his skin was darkening. A composer friend at Ischl, Richard Heuberger, begged him to consult a doctor, and Brahms consented, on condition that he should not be told ' anything unpleasant '.

The Ischl doctor accordingly diagnosed ' a mild jaundice ' and called in a Viennese specialist, who was staying nearby, to give a second opinion. They suggested to Brahms that he should take a Karlsbad cure, but to Heuberger they confided that Brahms was suffering from a very severe liver complaint from which there was little hope of recovery.

As the drinking of Karlsbad water at Ischl proved ineffective, Brahms was sent to Karlsbad to undergo the full cure. His friend Dr Fellinger accompanied him on the journey. He and other friends gave Brahms personal introductions to notable guests at Karlsbad and to the medical authorities there; and so he enjoyed congenial companionship and special facilities at the springs.

In October he returned to Vienna, ostensibly to pick up the threads of his professional life; but he was no longer his old resilient self. Even walking became an effort, and he was very glad to be taken for carriage drives by his friends. He kept up the fiction of ' a mild jaundice ' and even made whimsical allusions to his slimming figure. Whether he realised the true nature of his illness he never divulged, but as he had seen his father die of cancer of the liver, he can hardly have been unaware of the critical nature of his own complaint. Yet he persisted in maintaining an iron reserve on the subject, even when he began to feel really ill.

Brahms spent Christmas with the Fellingers, as so often before, and in January 1897 actually appeared on the concert platform, led thither by Joachim to receive a storm of applause after a performance of his string quintet in G. In early March he was taken to an orchestral concert given by the Gesellschaft der Musikfreunde, when he sat in the directors' box to listen to his fourth symphony conducted by Hans Richter. After each movement applause broke out, and at the very end, Brahms received the ovation of a lifetime from his host of Viennese admirers. As he stood to acknowledge the plaudits, tears were running down his cheeks. Everyone present must have felt that this was a mutual farewell.

Soon Brahms could no longer leave his house, and by the end of March he was bedridden. Every possible kindness and attention was shown to him by his still numerous friends and by the devoted Frau Truxa. Although he was utterly wretched at being unable to work and was in constant discomfort, he did not suffer acute pain. He sank rapidly. On the morning of April 3 1897 he breathed his last.

HOMAGE

All Vienna mourned his passing and he was accorded elaborate funeral ceremonies that would have done honour to a reigning monarch. They were entirely out of keeping with Brahms's own simple tastes, but one feature of the procession he would truly have appreciated. Twelve distinguished musicians and personal friends followed his coffin as torch-bearers. Among them were his fellow composer and former protégé Dvořák, and his disciple and young colleague Mandyczewski.

Representatives from musical centres in other countries came to Vienna to pay their last tribute. In Hamburg, the city of Brahms's birth, he was honoured in a manner that would have pleased him most of all. During the hour of the funeral, the ships in the harbour all lowered their flags to half mast.

Books in English about Brahms

Although Brahms never came to England, his music became well known here during the latter part of his lifetime, owing largely to the advocacy of his performer friends, particularly Joseph Joachim, Clara Schumann, Julius Stockhausen and George Henschel. He already had many English admirers, among whom was a sprinkling of musical scholars who later wrote about his life and works.

One of them, J A Fuller-Maitland (1856-1936), music critic of *The times* (1889-1911), was responsible for the publication of the very first book on Brahms in English. He edited and wrote a preface to *Johannes Brahms: a biographical sketch* by Hermann Deiters (T Fisher Unwin, 1888). Fuller-Maitland was himself a future biographer of Brahms and writer of the articles on the composer in the *Encyclopaedia Britannica* (fourteenth edition), and in the original edition of Grove's *Dictionary of music and musicians* (1879). The translator of the book was Rosa Newmarch, later well known as a writer of programme notes. Both Mrs Newmarch and Fuller-Maitland made additions to the English version of Deiters' sketch in order to include the works Brahms composed during the period of almost eight years that elapsed between the publication of the German original and the English translation. The author, Hermann Deiters (1833-1901), a German writer on music, whose most important work was the translation into German of the American A W Thayer's colossal *Life of Beethoven,* had known Brahms since their youth and had always kept in touch with him. He was thus well qualified to write what has since been termed ' the first authoritative biography of Brahms '. The preliminary section was published in Leipzig by Breitkopf & Härtel in 1880. The English translation is simply an abridgement of it, and although Deiters brought out a new, completed and revised edition in 1898 after Brahms's death, this latter was never translated into English. As a biography it has inevitably been superseded by later, more substantial works. Its actual value for present day readers is slight, but it is of interest historically in recording contemporary critical opinion of the works by the man whom the author considered ' by far the greatest composer of our time '.

Another ' biographical sketch ' of Brahms, published while he was still living, was written by W H Hadow (1859-1937), the distinguished educationist, and was included in his *Studies in modern music* (Seeley, 1895, eleventh impression, 1926). Admittedly it is less concerned with biography than with analysis and criticism of Brahms's musical style, and its value to the student of Brahms is historical rather than intrinsic, but it still retains a time honoured place in recent Brahms bibliographies.

SOURCES AND RECOLLECTIONS
The documents which have formed the principal basis of all subsequent studies of Brahms are the letters he exchanged with his friends, colleagues, publishers and performing musicians. This vast correspondence fills sixteen volumes published by the German Brahms Society (1907-22) and edited by various scholars. Only four series of the letters are available to English readers.

Before the first of these appeared, in 1909, came a book of personal reminiscences by two friends of Brahms's which itself consists largely of letters from the composer, held together by intervening sections of narrative and commentary: Albert Dietrich and J V Widmann, *Recollection of Johannes Brahms*, translated by Dora Hecht (Seeley, 1899). Dietrich (1829-1908), German composer and conductor, deals with the years 1853-86 and covers Brahms's activities in the Schumann circle up to the time of Schumann's death, then the composer's Detmold period and lastly his residence in Vienna. Widmann (1842-1911), Swiss poet and librettist of Moravian birth, writes of the period 1874-97, during which he and Brahms spent holidays together in Switzerland, Italy, Sicily and Austria; experiences that gave Widmann many opportunities of forming the sympathetic estimate of Brahms's character which he includes in the book. He also goes fully into the proposal for his own collaboration as the librettist of an opera which Brahms long considered writing; a project that was eventually given up by the composer after some years of discussion between the two men.

A smaller book of reminiscences, this time written originally in English, was first published in USA by George Henschel: *Personal recollections of Johannes Brahms* (Richard G Badger, Boston 1907). Henschel (1850-1934), German born baritone singer, composer and conductor, who settled in England and took British nationality, first met Brahms in 1874 at Cologne. He subsequently sang under his direction on many occasions and they became close friends. In 1876 the two spent a holiday together on the island of Rügen, where Henschel kept a journal which forms the core of his reminiscences. He republished the *Recollections* as Chapter V of his book *Musings and memories of a musician* (Macmillan, 1918) and they were finally reprinted in abridged form as part IV of his daughter Helen Henschel's *When soft voices die. A musical biography* (John Westhouse, 1944).

Another very intimate personal recollection of the composer is comprised in a chapter of thirty pages entitled ' Brahms ' in Eugenie Schumann's *Memoirs,* translated by Marie Busch (Heinemann, 1927), published simultaneously in USA as *The Schumanns and Johannes Brahms; the memoirs of Eugenie Schumann* (L MacVeagh, The Dial Press, 1927). The writer, born in 1851 as the fourth daughter of the composer Robert Schumann, had been closely acquainted with Brahms since her childhood and had studied piano with him. Her account of his method of teaching is especially interesting and her summing up of his character both shrewd and sympathetic.

LETTERS
The first section of Brahms's letters to appear in English was *Johannes Brahms: the Herzogenberg correspondence,* edited by Max Kalbeck, translated by Hannah Bryant (John Murray, 1909). The interchange of letters was carried on during the twenty one years from 1876 to 1897, and forms a fascinating record of the intimate friendship that existed between the Herzogenbergs, hus-

band and wife, and the composer. Elisabeth (née von Stockhausen), a good amateur pianist with a remarkably acute critical faculty, had been a pupil of Brahms's in Vienna before her marriage to Heinrich von Herzogenberg, conductor of the Bach Society in Leipzig and later teacher of composition in Berlin. Brahms used regularly to send his new compositions to the pair 'on approval' and often adopted their suggestions as to revisions. By far the greater number of the 281 letters in this collection are those to and from Elisabeth, who as a writer had an exquisitely light touch. Typical of her style is this extract from a letter she wrote to Brahms in 1890 after receiving from him the much revised version of his early trio in B major. 'I was strangely affected by your old new trio. Something within me protested against the remodelling. I felt you had no right to intrude your master touch on this lovable, if somewhat vague, production of your youth. . . . However, I recognised your inset in the first movement *instantly,* was completely disarmed and played on in a transport of delight. It is *beautiful* in its present form and I gladly leave it to the musical philologues to remonstrate with you. . . .' After her untimely death in 1892, Brahms, in writing to Heinrich, referred to her letters thus: 'I cherish those I have as, in the first place, one of the most precious memories of my life, and also for their intrinsic qualities of wit and temperament'. The editor of the correspondence, Max Kalbeck (1850-1921), a personal friend and keen partisan of Brahms, was the author of the 'standard' biography of Brahms (four volumes, 1904-14), which, although it has never been translated into English, has been drawn upon by writers on Brahms down to the present day.

Letters from and to Joseph Joachim, selected and translated by Nora Bickley, with a preface by J A Fuller-Maitland (Macmillan, 1914) contains only twenty five of the more than 500 letters he exchanged with his life long friend Brahms. Some of the letters to and from other people, especially Clara Schumann, are also of great interest in throwing sidelights upon Brahms's character and upon his capacity as a pianist. Many of the letters are of value, too, as sources of information on later nineteenth century musical life in England, where Joachim played annually for many years, either as soloist or with his famous quartet.

The most extensive collection of the Brahms correspondence available in English is *Letters of Clara Schumann and Johannes Brahms 1853-1896,* edited by Berthold Litzmann, with a preface by Marie Schumann and introduction by the translator (Edward Arnold, two volumes 1927). Even these two big volumes do not comprise the whole of the correspondence. Marie Schumann tells in her preface that her mother and Brahms agreed to the mutual return of their earlier letters and to the destruction of most of them, especially those from Clara to Brahms up to 1858. The number was still further reduced by means of selection and abridgements by the translator (A M Ludovici). Even so, this English version of the Clara Schumann-Brahms correspondence, incomplete though it is, forms an incomparable record of a long and intimate friendship between two outstanding musical personalities.

A reflection in miniature of this large compilation is provided by a small book published nearly thirty years later: *A passionate friendship, Clara Schumann and Brahms,* by Marguerite and Jean Alley, translated by Mervyn Savill (Edward Arnold, 1956). It is, as the authors state, only ' a selection of the most significant ' of the letters, here linked together by passages explaining their context. The book does not illuminate the actual nature of the ' passionate friendship ' any more clearly than does Litzmann's large scale edition of the letters, but to readers who have neither time nor opportunity for studying Litzmann, this little anthology gives at least some idea of the general tone of the correspondence.

The last section of the correspondence to appear in English was published in America. It was *Johannes Brahms and Theodor Billroth: letters from a musical friendship,* translated and edited by Hans Barkan (University of Oklahoma Press, Norman, Oklahoma, 1957). Billroth (1829-1894), a surgeon with a European reputation, a good amateur musician and a man of wide culture, was, like Brahms, a north German by birth. Their intimate friendship dates from 1867 when Billroth was appointed professor of surgery in Vienna. He was an enthusiast for Brahms's works, which the composer often submitted to him for criticism; he used to arrange performances of Brahms's chamber music at his own house, taking part himself as viola player. It was with Billroth that Brahms first went on holiday to Italy and Sicily. The letters consist largely of a lively interchange of opinions on music, art, literature and the theatre. The editor provides brief biographies of the letter writers and some interesting and unusual photographs of Brahms.

BIOGRAPHIES

From the first decade of the twentieth century onwards, biographies of Brahms and studies of his music by English and American writers, as well as English translations of those by foreign writers, have appeared in plenty. About half the books deal with both the life and the works, though in greatly varying proportions. They will be considered here before the more specialised studies of the works themselves.

Life and works: To one of the earliest full length biographies belongs the twofold distinction of having been written by a piano pupil of Brahms and of having remained, after more than sixty years, the standard English life of the composer: Florence May's *The life of Johannes Brahms* in two volumes (William Reeves, 1905). The author prepared a revised and corrected edition, but it was not issued owing to the difficulties of publishing during the 1914-18 war. Not until twenty five years after her death was the second edition seen through the press in 1948 by Ralph Hill.

Florence May (1844-1923) went in 1871, as a budding concert pianist, to study with Clara Schumann at Lichtental near Baden Baden. When, after a few months, the latter had to go away on concert tours, she arranged for her pupil to be taught by Brahms, who was living in the neighbourhood. She thus acquired an unrivalled opportunity for writing the sketch of Brahms's methods of teaching and performing which forms the prelude to the *Life*. The biography itself, the fruit of painstaking research, is balanced, detailed and fully documented, and is written with affection and enthusiasm in a pleasant leisurely style. Florence May makes no claim to have given 'technical' accounts of the compositions, but only to have tried to help music lovers to enjoy them. Many of her critical opinions are hardly valid today.

This large book had just been preceded by one of very small proportions: *Brahms* by Herbert Antcliffe, in Bell's 'Miniature series of musicians' (George Bell, 1905). Its fifty six pages are divided between brief studies of 'The life', 'The man and the artist' and 'The works'. An interesting inclusion is a detailed list of the melodic sources of Brahms's *Hungarian dances*. Some of the author's critical opinions are now so outdated as to make amusing reading at the present time.

The year 1905 saw the publication of yet one more book on Brahms, this time by an American writer and in a series published simultaneously in England and USA: J Lawrence Erb, *Brahms*, in 'The master musicians' (J M Dent; NY, E P Dutton, 1905, revised by the editor and printed in 1934). Although it had to be replaced in the same series over forty years later by a more up-to-date book which will be referred to later, it still remains eminently readable. The matter is exceptionally well presented. The continuous biographical narrative includes mention of each work as it was composed and the name of the publisher. Abstracts of the three sections ('Biography', 'Brahms the man', 'Brahms the musician') are printed in the list of contents so that the reader can obtain a bird's eye view of their substance for quick reference. The general summing up is reasoned, and the appraisal of the music sympathetic. The comprehensive bibliography is especially strong in point of American books and articles on Brahms.

The musical art of Brahms: Readers' demands for biographies of Brahms had evidently been satisfied for the time being by Florence May's exhaustive *Life*, for the two books that followed were concerned less with biography than with Brahms's art as a whole and his position in the musical world of his own day and later. First came H C Colles *Brahms*, in 'The music of the masters', edited by Wakeling Dry (John Lane, 1909; NY, Brentano's; second edition 1920). Here, biography is confined to a 'chronological table of the life'; the works are surveyed in eight chapters, each dealing with a single category, and a final chapter examines 'The position of Brahms'. Throughout the pages individual compositions are subjected to technical analysis and accompanied by music examples.

At the time he wrote the book Colles (1879-1943) was on the staff of *The times* as assistant music critic to Fuller-Maitland, whose own book on the composer was published three years later: *Brahms* by J A Fuller-Maitland (Methuen, 1911; NY, John Lane). It came out in 'The new library of music' edited by Ernest Newman, a series which included another 'classic' of similar calibre, R A Streatfield's *Handel* (1909). Fuller-Maitland devotes only one chapter to biography and to the study of Brahms's character; another to Brahms and his contemporaries, in which he deals very fully with the Wagner-Brahms-Liszt controversy, as well as with the influence that Schumann and Joachim exerted upon Brahms and his position in the musical world of his time. In a third chapter he examines the characteristics of his art, and each of the remaining six chapters is given to analysis and criticism of the compositions in their several categories. The chapter on the songs is especially detailed. Although the literary style is dated and the impassioned pleading for the acceptance of Brahms's compositions is now entirely superfluous, the book is genuinely enjoyable to read for its sympathetic appreciation and scholarly treatment of the music.

Another Brahms enthusiast of the same generation, Sir Charles Stanford (1852-1924) wrote a tiny monograph on the composer the following year. It was first published in USA: *Brahms* by C V Stanford, (NY, Frederck A Stokes, 1912; reissued in London by Murdoch in 1927 as one of the 'Mayfair biographies' and reprinted by Chappell in 1947). Written in unhurried and informal style it is a *multum in parvo* of great charm. The twenty four largish pages (unnumbered) are divided almost equally into two sections: 'Historical', comprising a discussion of the music for concert and theatre, the contrast between Brahms and Wagner and their respective artistic pedigrees and 'educational family trees'; and 'Biographical', which also includes some account of the compositions and a characterisation of Brahms himself. Little black and white drawings adorn the text throughout.

E Markham Lee's *Brahms: the man and his music* (Sampson Low, Marston, 1916) is both a biography and a study of the compositions, each category being treated in a separate chapter. The book is designed for non-expert readers and is 'popular' in character. Jeffrey Pulver's *Johannes Brahms* (Kegan Paul, Trench, Trubner; J Curwen & Sons, 1926), although undistinguished in literary style is informative in the extreme. The biographical section is packed so tightly with details and is so closely compressed that it lends itself better to reference than to continuous reading. The critical analysis of the composer whom Pulver considers 'intellectually, the most important figure in the whole history of music', is thoughtfully reasoned. Occasional chapters on 'classic, romantic and the New Germans', the Brahms-Wagner controversy, and Brahms's contemporaries round out the whole.

Before the appearance of the next biography by an English writer came three large scale works successively from Germany, Austria and USA. First was Walter Niemann's *Brahms*, translated by Catherine Alison Philips (NY, Knopf, 1929; Tudor Publishing Co, 1945). It had originally been published in Germany in 1920 and claimed to be 'the first critical biography' of Brahms. Part I, 'The life', also includes studies of Brahms as a man and as pianist, teacher and performer. In part II, which opens with a preliminary survey of Brahms's style, all the compositions are submitted to appraisal and analysis, especially of their expressive qualities, and to an examination of their context in the composer's life. The appendices include comprehensive lists of works in every branch of Brahms's output, creative and editorial. Walter Niemann (1876-1953) was, like Brahms, a north German of Holstein ancestry and a native of Hamburg. He persistently lays stress upon Brahms's north German traits, even ascribing all his personal characteristics, whether virtues or failings, to his 'Nordic' provenance; an idiosyncratic viewpoint oddly at variance with the prevailing objectivity of this reliable, broadly based study of the composer.

It was followed by a work of very different character: Richard Specht's *Johannes Brahms*, translated by Eric Blom (J M Dent; NY, E P Dutton, 1930). The opening chapter 'Pilgrimage in the Rhineland', in the style of an historical novel, gives an imaginary account of the youthful Brahms journeying on foot to his first meeting with the Schumanns. The ensuing biography is thrice interpolated by a chapter entitled 'Interlude of the work' (appraisal of compositions), and by other chapters relating to individual aspects of Brahms's activities. The writing is subjective, repetitious, highly emotional and over dramatised; a torrential flow of verbosity. Richard Specht (1870-1932), a Viennese writer on music, knew

Brahms personally during his last ten years and used to listen to him playing quietly in his own home. His firsthand account of the composer's style as pianist towards the end of his life and his vivid pen portraits of the distinguished members of Brahms's circle of intimate friends lend the book a certain individual cachet. Eric Blom's translation is masterly.

The year of the centenary of Brahms's birth saw the publication of a book which had been begun over thirty years earlier: Robert Haven Schauffler's *The unknown Brahms, his life, character and works, based on new material* (NY, Dodd Mead, 1933; sixth printing, Crown Publishers, 1940). The author, an American of Austrian extraction, made his first journey to Europe in 1902 to learn all he could about Brahms from people who had known him personally in any capacity. During the following years he paid fifteen more visits to Europe for the same purpose, interviewed 150 people in six countries and collected ' new and significant material ' from them which he embodied in his well planned, sincerely written book. The first section comprises a fascinating record of his musical pilgrimage. Following the biographical section are chapters devoted to aspects of the ' unknown ' Brahms. One, which ' represents the first attempt yet made by a biographer to explain, with the help of modern science, Brahms's cryptic love life ', lends the book a rather sensational tone. The study of the ' Profile of Brahms's musical style ' is sound and perceptive, although the analyses of individual compositions are inclined to be arbitrary. The critical apparatus in the appendices is first class.

In the same year, the music critic and editor Ralph Hill (1900-1950) published his *Brahms, A study in musical biography,* with introduction by Evelyn Howard-Jones (Dennis Archer, 1933). Designed for the general reader, it ' concentrates on a study of the composer *in broad outline,* showing the several conflicting sides of his character as displayed in his intercourse with his friends and acquaintances '. The biography is preluded by a survey of the nineteenth century musical scene which formed the background to Brahms's life, and by a study of romanticism in music and the arts. It is concluded by consideration of the place of Brahms in the hierarchy of symphonists, and of the sources of his musical style.

63

This book also serves as the basis of the same author's equally valuable *Brahms,* in the ' Great lives series ' (Duckworth, 1941; NY, A A Wyn, 1948).

A book which contained vital new material and was first published in German in 1934 is Karl Geiringer's *Brahms. His life and works,* translated by H B Weiner and Bernard Miall (Allen & Unwin, 1936; second edition, revised and enlarged, NY, Oxford University Press, 1947, and London, Allen & Unwin, 1948). This is a full length biography as well as a comprehensive study of the music. Geiringer (b 1899), had been appointed custodian of the Museum of the Gesellschaft der Musikfreunde in Vienna in 1930, in which capacity he was authorised to read the large number of letters received by Brahms from his family and friends, hitherto kept under seal in the museum and inaccessible to other investigators. Geiringer quotes frequently from these personal documents. which he considers ' far more vivid than any modern description could be ', in order ' to supplement the material of all previous books on Brahms and in particular to revise the estimate of the composer's character and psychological development'. Later writers on Brahms are greatly indebted to his dedicated research. The second edition has an appendix entitled ' Brahms writes letters ', comprising a selection of about thirty letters from Brahms to various friends, not previously available to English readers. More important is the discussion by Geiringer of compositions by Brahms which had not been discovered when the first edition of his book was printed twelve years previously.

Peter Latham's *Brahms,* in ' The master musicians ', new series edited by Eric Blom (Dent, 1948) replaces Lawrence Erb's book in the same series (1905) already mentioned. Although published over twenty years ago Latham's is the most recent sizeable biography of Brahms by an English writer. The author's careful scholarship, sympathetic approach to his subject and attractive literary style combine to make this a most enjoyable book. The complete catalogue of Brahms's works is particularly valuable. In the same year came John Culshaw's *Brahms: an outline of his life and music,* with a preface by Alec Robertson (Hinrichsen, 1948). Less space is devoted to biography than to the consideration of the music. Selected works in every category except solo songs and small scale choral pieces, are helpfully discussed and gramophone recordings of each are recommended. The projected booklets on all Brahms's major works, mentioned in the author's preface, have unfortunately never been issued.

A gap of several years separated this book from its immediate successor, an important monograph embodying recent research, first published at Frankfurt am Main in 1961 : Hans Gal's *Johannes Brahms, his work and personality,* translated from the German by Joseph Stein (Weidenfeld & Nicholson, 1963; NY, Alfred Knopf). Gal (b 1891) was ideally equipped for his task, having studied under Eusebius Mandyczewski (1857-1929), a renowned musical scholar and archivist who was an intimate friend of Brahms during the last twenty years of the composer's life. Gal later collaborated with him in publishing Breitkopf & Härtel's edition of Brahms's complete works, and enjoyed countless opportunities for discussing with him every possible matter concerning Brahms. His book is the outcome of an ' intensive, lifelong engagement and a thorough acquaintance with Brahms's work '. It is an authoritative, discerning study of Brahms, the man, his setting, achievements and methods, the whole complex subject matter being viewed in perspective. This scholarly survey is of absorbing interest from beginning to end.

THE MUSIC

Among studies of Brahms's music are a few which embrace his entire output rather than any specialised branch of it. Earliest is the American Daniel Gregory Mason's *From Grieg to Brahms* (NY, Outlook Company, 1902; new and enlarged edition, 1927), in which a section of twenty seven pages is devoted to a general, though reasonably detailed appraisal of Brahms's work. This author's book on the chamber music will be considered later. W H Hadow's ' Brahms and the classical tradition ' was printed in his *Collected essays* (pp 135-147) (Oxford University Press, 1928). The high flown literary style and abundance of eulogy make this essay something of a period piece but it contains many undeniably sound judgements.

A book that by reason of its gigantic scope occupies a unique position in Brahms literature was published in instalments by Edwin

Evans, Senior (1844-1923): *Historical descriptive and analytical account of the entire works of Johannes Brahms* (William Reeves, four volumes 1912-36 NY, Scribner). It comprises 1,500 pages and more than 1,000 music examples and tables. Every work is submitted to close analysis and accompanied by biographical, historical and general information and there is a wealth of indices and appendices. In effect, the whole of Brahms's output is submitted to intensive scientific dissection. Each of the four volumes is 'self contained and a complete textbook on its particular subject'. Volume I (vocal and choral works) also includes the German words and English translations of all the songs (or at least of some of the verses). Volumes II and III, covering chamber and orchestral music, respectively treat works up to op 67 and those from op 68 to op 120. Volume IV is devoted to the piano music, solo and duet, as well as the two concertos, Brahms's arrangements of his own and of other composers' works, and his organ music. As a work of reference the whole is a triumph of organisation that inspires respect and gratitude in its users.

CHORAL MUSIC

There is no single book in English dealing exclusively with Brahms's large scale choral orchestral works. One which examines this lesser known branch of his art, which is only scantily treated in most books on the composer is Sophie Drinker's *Brahms and his women's choruses,* with a preface by Karl and Irene Geiringer (Merion, Pa, 1952). Dr Drinker (1888-1967), an amateur singer, pursued her researches in Hamburg, where the Hamburg Ladies' Choir, founded by Brahms before he was thirty, had been the original inspiration for his writing this type of composition. She succeeded in tracing and collecting many of the partbooks and some of the diaries belonging to original members of the choir and wrote her study on the basis of these rare documents. The book contains a mass of interesting information on domestic music making in nineteenth century Germany. It also gives particulars of the Drinker Library of Choral Music by Brahms and other composers, edited and supplied with English words by her husband Henry S Drinker for use by the Westminster Choral

College at the University of Princeton NJ. It is, perhaps, one of the most unusual books on Brahms.

VOCAL MUSIC

The solo songs and duets are examined in great detail by Max Friedlaender (1852-1934) in his *Brahms's lieder, an introduction to the songs for one and two voices,* translated by C Leonard Leese (Oxford University Press, 1928). The study, which was first published in Germany in 1922, is pre-eminently a book of reference and is splendidly indexed. It includes not only a musical analysis of every song but also the history of its composition, the source of the words, deviations (if any) from the printed texts, names of publishers, contemporary opinions of the songs, remarks on Brahms's style as a songwriter and especially his reactions to German folksong. The author, who knew Brahms personally, was himself a singer and also a specialist on Schubert.

ORCHESTRAL MUSIC

The two earliest single studies of the orchestral music appeared in the 'Musical pilgrim series'. The first was E Markham Lee's *Brahms's orchestral works* (Oxford University Press, 1931), which covers the six that preceded the symphonies: the two serenades, the 'Haydn' variations, the two overtures and the violin concerto. Analyses with music examples are provided for each work, the most detailed being that of the 'Haydn' variations. The notes on the *Academic festival overture* are accompanied by the first few bars of each of the student songs incorporated therein. The second 'Pilgrim' was P A Browne's *Brahms: the symphonies* (OUP, 1933). The introduction contains a reasoned discussion of Brahms as a symphonist, his relationship to Beethoven, the special idiosyncrasies of his use of form and his methods of orchestration. Each symphony is fully analysed, with many music examples, dates of composition and of first performances. These two 'Pilgrims', though small in size, are substantial in content and very practical in use.

They were followed by a full length study of the symphonies by the conductor and composer Julius Harrison (1885-1963): *Brahms and his four symphonies* (Chapman & Hall, 1939). The preliminary

67

chapters constitute a penetrating survey of the formation and growth of Brahms's style in general, with reference also to branches of his art other than the orchestral. The symphonies themselves are subjected to minute analysis. Harrison owns to a ' passion for analysis ', and his book is designed for ' a vast musical public that has not only a large heart to respond to the beauty of all good music, but in addition, an intelligent head to appreciate the subtleties of effect and great technical skill evinced by a composer of genius '. The enthusiasm he displays for the music is not untempered by criticism.

After an interval of seven years came perhaps the strangest study in all Brahms literature: a highly subjective pamphlet entitled *Brahms and Keats; a parallel,* by Charles Neider (NY, Orion Press, 1946). The parallel drawn is between Keats's *Ode to a nightingale* and the *Andante sostenuto* of Brahms's first symphony. While declaiming the ode to the accompaniment of a gramophone recording of the andante, the author of the pamphlet thought he detected formalistic similarities between these respective creations of the ' classical romantic ' poet and composer. He presents parallel tabular analyses of the two works and suggests that Brahms might possibly have used the ode consciously as the structural background to the andante. As no documentary evidence exists to prove that Brahms even knew the ode, the pamphlet carries no conviction, but as a piece of imaginative writing it is not unattractive.

All the orchestral works of Brahms, including the four concertos, are examined by John Horton in his *Brahms orchestral music* (BBC Music Guides, 1968). Besides the discussion of each individual work, the history of its origin, and its relationship to the composer's other productions, there are separate sections dealing with ' Brahms the composer ' and ' Brahms and the orchestra '. This is a compact, expertly written little book with beautifully printed music examples.

CHAMBER MUSIC

The four available studies of the chamber music are alike in providing series of analyses of the twenty four works in this category, but they are written from very different standpoints and with differing artistic aims. D F Tovey's ' Brahms's chamber music ' was first published as an article in Cobbett's two volume *Cyclopedic survey of chamber music*, 1929, and was reprinted posthumously in D F Tovey *Essays and lectures on music* (pp 220-270) collected, with an introduction by Hubert Foss (OUP, 1949). In his approach to the subject, Tovey (1875-1940), a trained philosopher and a professor of music, blended the severely technical with the musically practical. His knowledge of music was cyclopedic, and as he had taken part as pianist in concert performances of Brahms's music with Joseph Joachim as partner, he had inherited some of the direct Brahms tradition of interpretation. The content of his essay is of incalculable value; his 'allusive, talkative prose style' (to quote Foss), his scintillating wit, scholarly digressions and paradoxes, combine to make the reading of his pages a thrilling and stimulating experience.

The next two studies came from USA. The first is from a lawyer and amateur musical scholar who describes himself as 'a Philadelphia disciple of Brahms'. *The chamber music of Johannes Brahms*, by Henry S Drinker Jr (1880-1965) (Philadelphia, Elkan Vogel, 1932) was prepared in the form of programme notes for the performance in Philadelphia of all Brahms's chamber music on the centenary of his birth (1933). In addition to the very full notes on each of the twenty four works, the book contains a sketch of Brahms's life and essays on his music as a totality and on the characteristics of his style. It is a sensitively written study.

Only six months later, Daniel Gregory Mason brought out *The chamber music of Brahms* (formerly published by the Macmillan Company, NY, 1933; reprinted with correction, J W Edwards, Ann Arbor, 1950; sole agent, Hinrichsen Edition). Mason (1873-1934), composer, pianist and university lecturer, came of an American family of musicians. He was a nephew of William Mason (1829-1908), a piano pupil of Liszt's when Brahms first visited him at Weimar, who later played in the world première of Brahms's trio in B major, op 8, in New York in 1855. Daniel Mason felt an especial sympathy with Brahms's music, about which he writes with great zest and skill, in an 'allusive, talkative style' that faintly recalls Tovey's. The searching analyses and general criticisms of every work are illustrated by 100 hand written music examples and by three facsimiles of pages from the original manuscripts.

The same year saw an addition to the 'Musical pilgrim series': H C Colles *The chamber music of Brahms* (Oxford University Press, 1933). Like H S Drinker, Colles wrote his set of analyses as programme notes for concerts in the centenary year. He included a work which is omitted from the three books just surveyed; namely, the early scherzo movement which Brahms contributed to the composite sonata for violin and piano written by Schumann, Dietrich and himself as a surprise for Joachim in 1853. In a preamble Colles describes the development of Brahms's style and the relationship of the chamber music to other branches of his output. This book though small in format is remarkably complete.

PIANO MUSIC

On the piano music there is only one exhaustive book: William Murdoch's *Brahms; with an analytical study of the complete piano-forte works* (Rich and Cowan, 1933, reprinted 1938). It is comprehensive indeed, opening with a biography of Brahms and a summing up of his character and achievement, and going on to survey, in addition to the music for piano solo and duet and the two concertos, all the chamber music in which the piano takes part. William Murdoch (1888-1942), an Australian by birth, was a well known solo pianist and a member of the English quartet named 'The Chamber Music Players'. In his preface he remarks that 'my sole reason for writing this book has been that I wanted to': a statement that is borne out by the enthusiastic, lively tone of the study. His critical opinions are well balanced and he gives some helpful advice on performing technique.

Editions of Brahms's music

At the time of Brahms's death in 1897 all the compositions that he himself intended for publication were already in print. Only his very last work, the set of eleven choral preludes for organ, which he completed during the year before his death, had to be published posthumously. It came out as op 122 in 1902.

There were, however, a few lesser works by Brahms still remaining to be published: either those which had never seen print or others which had appeared only in ephemeral publications. They were issued sporadically between 1906 and 1926 by the Deutsche Brahms Gesellschaft (German Brahms Society), Berlin. This heterogeneous little collection of nine items consists of five original compositions, cadenzas to a Beethoven concerto, an orchestration of a song by Schubert, a set of folksongs arranged for solo voice and piano, and Brahms's one literary effort: an anthology of quotations from great writers which he compiled from boyhood onwards under his occasional pseudonym 'Young Kreisler' (a name he adopted from one of E T A Hoffmann's characters). In recent years a few more relics have been discovered and printed. Each of these posthumous publications, except the anthology, is included in its respective category in the classified list of editions to follow.

Thematic catalogues
Brahms's output as a whole is fully documented in a series of thematic catalogues. The first of these appeared during his lifetime: *Thematisches Verzeichnis der bisher im Druck erschienenen Werke von Johannes Brahms* (Simrock, 1887). It comprises works only as far as op 101. The next edition, dated 1897, goes up to op

121, and the succeeding, progressively enlarged editions of 1902, 1904, 1907 and 1910 are as complete as was possible at the respective dates. These catalogues were all printed in German.

In 1956 a revised edition based on the Simrock catalogue was published in English. This was the *Thematic catalog of the collected works of Brahms,* an enlarged edition, edited with foreword by Joseph Braunstein (Ars Musica Press, Omega Music Corporation, NY). It includes all the works discovered since the previous editions and may be considered the most practical catalogue at the present time, although, unlike the German editions, it does not mention all the arrangements of Brahms's works beyond those made by the composer himself.

Excellent lists of the works are given in some of the English biographies of the composer, notably those by Florence May, J A Fuller-Maitland, William Murdoch, Peter Latham and Hans Gal. A most helpful guide in this sphere is O E Deutsch's long article ' The first editions of Brahms ', published serially in *The music review,* May 1940, 122-141 and August 1940, 255-278. It is wide in scope, embracing all Brahms's creative production, as well as his activity as arranger of his own works and of those by other composers, and his editorship of important collected editions of great masters. The precise and detailed information that Deutsch gives on the first editions themselves forms the centrepiece of his survey of the publication of Brahms's output from 1852, when the nineteen year old composer was writing pot-boilers for printing under an assumed name, until recent times, when all his copyrights had expired and his music was being reissued by innumerable publishers.

Brahms's publishers

The publishing of Brahms's compositions during his lifetime was undertaken by some ten firms in all. Chief among them were Simrock of Bonn, who were the original publishers of sixty eight works, and who transferred to their catalogue in 1880 the fourteen works first published by Breitkopf & Härtel of Leipzig from 1853-1866. Peters, also of Leipzig, published only five works, but in taking over the Swiss publisher Rieter-Biedermann of Winterthur and Leipzig in 1917, they acquired from this firm the copyrights of the twenty two works issued by them in 1861-71. From 1927 onwards, Simrock, and their English assignees, Alfred Lengnick of London, brought out a new 'complete' edition of Brahms, many numbers of which are now out of print. In any case, the edition was seriously diminished in stature by the almost simultaneous appearance of the Complete Edition.

THE COMPLETE EDITION

This monumental publication was sponsored by the Viennese Gesellschaft der Musikfreunde and was based on the authentic reference copies in their possession. Comprising twenty six volumes, it was entitled *Johannes Brahms, sämtliche Werke, Ausgabe der Gesellschaft der Musikfreunde in Wien* (Breitkopf & Härtel, 1926-28). It was edited jointly by Brahms's friend Eusebius Mandyczewski and the latter's former pupil Hans Gal. They carried out their work according to the very highest standards of musical scholarship, basing their readings on the autographs, the first editions, and in many instances on Brahms's own revised copies. Dr Gal was responsible for volumes I-VII and IX, X which cover orchestral and chamber music, and Mandyczewski for volumes XI-XXVI, comprising choral, solo vocal, piano and organ music. All these volumes are dated either 1926 or 1927; only volume VIII bears neither a date nor an editor's name. An invaluable collection, it remains the most authoritative edition of Brahms, even though, owing to subsequent finds of early works, it is now only nominally 'complete'. Moreover, of all the many arrangements (for piano solo or duet, orchestra, etc) that Brahms made of his own works, only a few are included. Among these are the alternative versions, for two pianos, of the piano quintet in F minor op 34B, and of the 'Haydn' variations for orchestra op 56B, the theme and variations from the string sextet in B flat op 18, arranged for piano solo, and three of the Hungarian dances arranged for orchestra.

Other editions

In the following lists, the letters CE and a roman numeral in brackets after the title denote the volume of the Complete Edition in which the respective work or group of works is printed. Alternative editions for practical purposes are given whenever such exist. The general principle of selection may be outlined as follows: the historical interest of the editor or arranger as a famous performer or teacher; the fact that a work may not be otherwise available at present; the interest of an arrangement, in an unusual but convenient medium. All editions are in score unless otherwise stated, and the word ' by ' is here equivalent to ' edited by '. Publishers' names are given in full except for the following:

Boosey	=Boosey & Hawkes (London; Hawkes Pocket Scores)
B&H	=Breitkopf & Härtel (Leipzig, Wiesbaden. London, British and Continental Music Agencies)
DBG	=Deutsche Brahms Gesellschaft
Eul	=Eulenburg (miniature scores by Wilhelm Altmann)
LPS	=Lea Pocket Scores (UE, NY, London) Reprints from the Complete Edition
L	=Lengnick
OUP	=Oxford University Press
Ric	=Ricordi (Milan, London)
RB	=Rieter-Biedermann (Winterthur and Leipzig)
S/C	=Schirmer/Chappell (NY, London)
S/L	=Simrock/Lengnick (Bonn, London)
Sch	=Schirmer (NY)
Southern	=Southern Music Publishing Company (NY)
UE	=Universal Edition (Vienna and London)
WPV	=Wiener Philharmonischer Verlag (Vienna) (Philharmonia pocket scores)

Where no town is given, the place of publication is London. The place of publication and the editor's christian name are omitted when either recurs several times in succession. Publishers' addresses are most readily available in the *British catalogue of music* (published by the British National Bibliography), which is to be found in major public libraries throughout the world. Besides the addresses of all British music publishers, this catalogue includes those of leading American firms and those of many European firms who have branches or agencies in London. DLCM denotes the Drinker Library of Choral Music (c/o the Free Library of

Philadelphia, Logan Square, Philadelphia, Pa 19103), a collection of choral and vocal works which includes a fair number by Brahms, all provided with new English translations by Henry S Drinker. Copies are available through the Association of American Choruses, Westminster Choir College, Princeton, NJ.

A complete index of first lines and titles of all the choral and vocal compositions is appended to the list of works included in J A Fuller-Maitland's study *Brahms*.

Vocal works
Sacred

Ein Deutsches requiem op 45: (words from Luther's bible), for solo voices, choir and orchestra (CE XVII). Miniature scores, with English translation of the text by R H Benson (Eul), and without editor's name (WPV). Vocal scores, with English translation by W G Rothery, organ accompaniment by John E West, preface by Ernest Newman (Novello); with English translation by the Bishop of Oxford and Steuart Wilson and organ accompaniment by C Palmer (OUP); with English translation by E M Traquair and R H Benson (Peters/Hinrichsen, NY) and in DLCM. With accompaniment arranged for piano four hands (or two pianos) by Brahms, by Leonard van Camp (Sch). This last named was the version used for the first (private) performance in London in 1871 at 35 Wimpole Street, the house of Lady Thompson, the wife of a distinguished physician, who herself played as duettist with Cipriani Potter, the octogenarian principal of the Royal Academy of Music.

Ave Maria op 12: for women's voices and orchestra or organ (CE XIX). Vocal score with organ (S/L).

Begräbnisgesang (*Funeral hymn*) op 13: for mixed choir and wind ensemble (CE XIX). Vocal score with English translation by E M Lockwood (S/L), and in DLCM.

Triumphlied (*Triumphal hymn*) op 55: with words from the *Revelation of St John* chapter 19, for baritone solo, double choir and orchestra (CE XVIII), arranged for piano (four hands) by Brahms (S/L).

Secular

Rinaldo (Goethe) op 50: cantata for tenor solo, male voice choir and orchestra (CE XVIII). Vocal score with English translation by J Powell Metcalfe (S/L), and in DLCM.

Rhapsodie (Goethe) op 53: for alto solo, male choir and orchestra (CE XIX). Miniature scores (Eul and WPV). Vocal scores with English translations by R H Benson (S/L) and by W G Rothery (Novello), and in DLCM.

Schicksalslied (*Song of destiny*—Hölderlin) op 54; for choir and orchestra (CE XIX.) Miniature score (WPV); vocal score with English translation by J Troutbeck (Novello).

Nänie (*Noenia, dirge*—Schiller) op 82: for choir and orchestra (CE XIX). Vocal score with English version by L Young (Novello); with German words and English translation by Mrs J P Morgan (Peters), and in DLCM.

Gesang der Parzen (*Song of the Fates*) op 89; for six part choir and orchestra (CE XIX). Miniature score (WPV); vocal score with English translation by Mrs Natalie Macfarren (Peters), and in DLCM.

Works for choir with instrumental accompaniment

Psalm 13, ' How long, O Lord' op 27: for women's voices and organ, or piano (CE XX). Vocal scores by Stainton de B Taylor (Hinrichsen) and C Lefebvre (Galaxy Music Corporation, NY).

Geistliches Lied (Paul Flemming) op 30: for mixed choir and organ, or piano (CE XX). Vocal score by Kurt Soldan, English translation by Walter E Buszin (Peters) and in DLCM.

Four partsongs op 17: for women's voices, two horns and harp (CE XIX). Vocal score with English translation by N Macfarren (S/L). No 2 is ' Come away, Death ', and No 4 ' Ossian's song from Fingal '.

Tafellied, Dank der Damen (To the ladies) op 93b: drinking glee for six part choir and piano (CE XX). Vocal score with English version by W Wager (Sch).

Works for unaccompanied choir (all in CE XXI)

Marienlieder (*Hymns to the Virgin*) op 22: for four part mixed voices. Score with English translation by Edward Oxenford (B&H); German words only (Peters). Six of the seven songs are in DLCM in their original versions for women's voices.

Two motets op 29: for five part mixed voices. Vocal score with German and English words (Peters). The first is based on the chorale

76

' Es ist das Heil uns kommen her '; the second uses words from Psalm 51. Both are fugal in treatment.

Three sacred choruses op 37: for women's voices, with latin words from the Liturgy (Peters) and with English words by E Oxenford (B&H).

Two motets op 74: for mixed choir. The first has words by Luther. Vocal scores, with English translations by N Macfarren (Simrock), L Baugh (L), W Wager (Sch) and A G Latham in an edition by W G Whittaker (OUP).

Fest- und Gedenksprüche op 109: for eight part mixed choir. With biblical words. Vocal score with the English text adapted by Mrs J P Morgan (S/L); also issued as *Three festival anthems,* with German and English words, the latter by Jean Lunn (Peters) and in DLCM.

Three motets op 110: for four and eight part choir. Vocal scores with English translation by A G Latham edited by W G Whittaker (OUP); with English version by J Lunn (Peters) and in DLCM. The words are biblical. No 3 is based on the chorale ' Wenn wir in höchsten Nöten sein ', well known from Bach's settings.

Five songs op 41: for four part men's choir. Vocal score with English words by E Oxenford (B&H), and with German words (Peters). The songs are military in character.

Three vocal pieces op 42: for six part mixed choir. Vocal score with English words by Astra Desmond (Cranz). No 2 is the well known ' Vineta ' (Wilhelm Müller), descriptive of a submerged city whose church bells are still sounding. No 3 is ' Darthulas Grabgesang ' (a dirge), by Ossian.

Twelve songs and romances op 44: for women's voices, SSA. Vocal score with English translation by Constance Bache (Stanley Lucas, Weber). In two sets of six each. Nos 1-4 of the second set are poems from Paul Heyse's ' Jungbrunnen '. Seven of these songs are in DLCM.

Seven songs op 62: for mixed choir. Vocal score with English translation by N Macfarren (Peters). Nos 1 and 2 on poems from A von Arnim and C Brentano's *Des Knaben Wunderhorn,* Nos 3-6, from P Heyse's ' Jungbrunnen '. No 4, ' Dein Herzlein mild ', and no 6, ' Es geht ein Wehen ', both in DLCM.

Six songs and romances op 93a: for four part mixed choir. Vocal scores with English translations by Mrs J P Morgan (s/l) and Elliot Forbes (Sch). No 3, 'Mädchenlied', with words from the Serbian, was later published as a solo song, op 95 no 1.

Five vocal pieces op 104: for mixed choir. Vocal score with English translation by Mrs J P Morgan (s/l) and in DLCM. Nos 1 and 2 on poems by F Rückert, both entitled 'Nachtwache'. The second, 'Ruhn sie?', was sung at Brahms's funeral in 1897.

Dem dunklen Schoss der heil'gen Erde (from Schiller's *Lied von der Glocke*) op posth: for mixed choir. Only in CE.

Canons (all in CE XXI)

Thirteen canons op 113: for three, four and six women's voices. Vocal score with English words by F Corder (Peters). The poems are by Goethe, Rückert, Eichendorff and Hoffman von Fallersleben, and are all in DLCM.

Three canons: for four women's voices. No 1 is 'Mir lächelt kein Frühling' and no 2 is 'Grausam erweiset sich Amor' (Goethe), both without opus number, in DLCM. No 3 is 'O wie sanft' (Daumer), op posth. No 3 was first published by DBG in 1908.

Two canons: for four mixed voices. 'Töne, lindernder Klang' is without opus number in DCLM and 'Zu Rauch' op posth.

Canon, for soprano and alto ('Wann, wann?'—Uhland): Without opus number.

Canon, for voice and viola ('Sprüch'—Hoffmann von Fallersleben) op posth.

Choir

Folksong settings for choir (all in CE XXVI)

Fourteen folksongs: for four part choir, in two books. Nos 1-7 and 8-14 (Peters), with English words by E Oxenford (B&H).

Eight German folksongs op posth: for four part choir (B&H).

Other folksong settings in this medium are included in collections for solo voice with piano. They are nos 29-32 of *Neue Volkslieder*, by Max Friedlaender (DBG), and nos 43-49 of *Forty nine German folksongs* (s/l) and in DLCM, which are designated 'with four part chorus ad lib'. No 49, 'Verstohlen geht der Mond auf', was originally used by Brahms for the second movement of his first piano sonata.

Folksongs for women's voices unaccompanied: arranged by Johannes Brahms, by Vernon Gotwals and Philip Keppler (' Smith College music Archives ' no XV, Northampton, Mass, USA). With introductory notes on the authenticity of the songs, some of which duplicate Brahms's solo songs. The volume contains an index of all the Brahms material in the Drinker Library of Choral Music. (Not in CE.)

Works for vocal quartet (SATB) with piano accompaniment (all in CE XX).

Brahms composed a large number of his smaller choral works in response to the current demand for this kind of music for performance in domestic circles; a form of recreation much cultivated in Germany in his day. This type of active music making having been displaced in recent times by passive listening to gramophone and radio, the Brahms choral music has fallen into neglect and much of it has unfortunately been allowed to go out of print.

Kleine Hochzeitskantate (Little wedding cantata—Gottfried Keller) op posth : for vocal quartet and organ (or piano), (CE only).

Three quartets op 31 : vocal score with English translation by W G Rothery (Novello); with German words (S/L). No 1 is Goethe's ' Wechsellied zum Tanze '.

Liebeslieder op 52 : waltzes for piano four hands with voices *ad lib.* Vocal scores with English words by N Macfarren (S/L), by W G Rothery (Novello), by E M Lockwood (L), and in DLCM; with German words (Peters). Brahms arranged a suite of nine waltzes for small orchestra at the request of Ernst Rudorff for performance in Berlin in 1870. This was edited from Brahms's own manuscript in 1938 by Wilhelm Weismann (Peters). (Not in CE.)

Neue Liebeslieder (Fifteen waltzes) op 65 : (as above). Vocal scores with English words by N Macfarren (S/L), by A G Latham in an edition by W G Whittaker (OUP), and with English translation by George Barker (L), and in DLCM. Brahms sanctioned the publication of both these sets of waltzes as piano duets without the voices, respectively as op 52a and 65a. (*See also Piano duets.*)

Three quartets op 64 : with poems by Schiller, Daumer and Sternau. Vocal score with German words (Peters and S/L).

Four quartets op 92: with English translation by Mrs J P Morgan (s/l); with German words (Peters). No 4 is Goethe's 'Warum?'.

Zigeunerlieder (*Gipsy songs*) op 103: from the Hungarian of H Conrat. Vocal scores with English translations by Mrs J P Morgan (s/l) and E M Lockwood (s/l). By W G Whittaker with English words by A G Latham (OUP), and in DLCM. (*See also Solo songs.*)

Six quartets op 112: the words of nos 3-6 are also *Zigeunerlieder*. Vocal score with English words by F Corder (Peters).

Vocal duets, with piano accompaniment (all in CE XXII)

Three duets op 20: for soprano and contralto. *Four duets* op 61: for soprano and contralto. *Five duets* op 66: for soprano and contralto. All with English translations by N Macfarren (s/l). *Four duets* op 28: for contralto and baritone, with English translations by W G Rothery (Novello). No 1 is Eichendorff's 'Die Nonne und der Ritter' and no 3 is 'Es rauschet das Wasser' (Goethe).

Four ballades and romances op 75: with English translations by N Macfarren (s/l). No 1, 'Edward', for contralto and tenor, is a setting of a Scottish ballad, from Herder's collection of folk poetry, which had already inspired the composition of Brahms's first ballade for piano op 10. No 2, 'Gueter Rat', is for soprano, as is also no 3, 'So lass uns wandern'. No 4, 'Walpurgisnacht', is for two sopranos.

Five songs and romances op 84: for one or two voices, are dialogue songs, not genuine duets. They are listed here with the solo songs in CE XXV.

Songs with opus number

Brahms composed just over two hundred solo songs with piano accompaniment, using a wide variety of verse by major and minor poets, as well as traditional and folk poems. He also arranged nearly one hundred folksongs for solo voice and piano. This whole production occupies the last four volumes of CE:

Vol XXIII: op 3, 6, 7, 14, 19, 32, 33
Vol XXIV: op 43, 46-49, 57-59, 63
Vol XXV: op 69-72, 84-86, 91, 94-97
Vol XXVI: op 105-107, 121, all the folksongs, and *Mondnacht* and *Regenlied*.

The songs are reproduced, complete, in eight of the Lea Pocket Scores (UE), with new English translations by Henry S Drinker.

Of other editions, the most complete is published by Peters (Leipzig and London), in four books without an editor's name. Only book II has English words, by an unnamed translator. No folksongs are included. The collection is arranged in arbitrary manner, the individual sets (opus groups) being broken up and divided between the four books, though admittedly in chronological order in each book.

Among incomplete editions the largest is *Ein- und zwei-stimmige Lieder und Gesänge,* with English translations by Paul England, Mrs Natalie Macfarren and Mrs John P Morgan of NY (S/L), which covers twenty three out of the total thirty two individual groups : some 129 solo songs in all and forty two of the folksongs. The four sets of duets, op 20, 61, 66 and 75, also included in the edition, have already been listed here as vocal duets. The solo songs in the collection are as follows :

Six songs op 3 : including ' Liebestreu '. *Six songs* op 7 : four with words by Eichendorff. *Five poems* op 19 : nos 4 and 5 are ' Der Schmied ' and 'An eine Aeolsharfe '. *Four songs* op 46; no 4 is 'An die Nachtigall '. *Five songs* op 47 : including ' O Liebliche Wangen '. *Seven songs* op 48. *Five songs* op 49 : no 4, ' Wiegenlied ' arranged for piano by Percy Grainger (Sch); arranged for harp by C Salzedo (Elkan Vogel, Philadelphia); adapted for piano by Gerald Moore (OUP). Nine songs op 69 : the poems largely translations from Czech, Slovak, Serbian and Spanish. *Four songs* op 70. *Five songs* op 71 : no 5 is ' Minnelied '. *Five songs* op 72. *Five songs and romances* op 84 : for one or two voices; those ' for two voices ' are dialogue songs, *eg* ' Vergebliches Ständchen '. *Six songs* op 85. *Six songs* op 86 : of which no 3, ' Nachtwandler ', in facsimile by O E Deutsch and Max Kalbeck (UE), and no 2 is ' Feldeinsamkeit '. *Two songs* op 91 : for contralto and viola or cello, transcribed for piano solo by Harold Bauer (Sch). *Five songs* op 94 : no 4 of which, ' Sapphische Ode ', is in facsimile by Deutsch and Kalbeck (UE). *Seven songs* op 95. *Four songs* op 96 : no 2 is ' Wir wandelten '. *Six songs* op 97. *Eight gipsy songs* op 103 : comprising nos 1-7 and no 11 of the vocal quartets (*Zigeunerlieder*), here arranged by Brahms for

81

solo voice (also published separately with English translations by Mrs J P Morgan (Schott)). *Five songs* op 105: include 'Wie Melodien zieht es mir' and 'Immer leise wird mein Schlummer'. *Five songs* op 106: no 3 is 'Es hing der Reif im Lindenbaum'. *Five songs* op 107: of which no 3 is 'Das Mädchen spricht'. *Vier ernste Gesänge* op 121: for bass voice, with biblical words. *Facsimiles*: *a*) from the original in the archives of the Gesellschaft der Musikfreunde (Drei Masken Verlag, Simrock), and *b*) from a calligraphic manuscript by Hermann Zapf printed for members of the Maximilian Society (August Osterrieth, Frankfurt). The four songs also published for contralto voice with English by Paul England (s/L); for high and low voice by C Deis with English words by Willis Wager (s/c); and for contralto or baritone, with English and German words, orchestrated by Malcolm Sargent (OUP). *Forty nine folksongs*: in seven books (the seventh, with chorus, not included. *See under Folksong settings for choir*).

A smaller collection comprising about fifty songs published separately in individual opus groups is provided with English translations by W G Rothery (Novello). A few of them duplicate some in the edition listed above. The contents of this Novello collection are: *Six songs* op 3; *Eight songs and romances* op 14: largely with traditional poems; *Five poems* op 19; *Nine songs* op 32: (in two sets, nos 1-4 and 5-9), with words by G F Daumer and Platen, no 9 of which is 'Wie bist du, meine Königin'; *Four songs* op 43: no 2 of which, 'Mainacht', is published in facsimile by O E Deutsch and M Kalbeck (UE), and no 4. 'Das Lied von Herrn Falkenstein', is orchestrated by Brahms's friend Richard Heuburger (R/B). The whole of this op 43 also with English words by R H Benson and Constance Bache (R/B). *Four songs* op 46; *Four songs* op 47; *Seven songs* op 48; and *Five songs* op 49 (*see above* for details of op 49 no 4, 'Wiegenlied').

Groups of songs which are either omitted from the two last named collections, or which are issued by other publishers and in English versions by different translators, are as follows: *Six songs* op 3: with English by Elsa d'Esterre Keeling and Paul England (B&H). *Six songs* op 6: with German and English words, the latter by E Ebertz (L); also edited by A Visetti (Augener) and by A

Randegger with English words by F Mansfield (Novello). *Six songs* op 7: English by E d'E Keeling (B&H). *Fifteen romances from Tieck's Magelone* op 33: in five sets of three songs, with English translations by Andrew Lang and R H Benson (R/B). *Eight songs* op 57: (in two sets, nos 1-4 and 5-8), with poems by Daumer, and *Eight songs* op 58: (in two sets, nos 1-4 and 5-8); both these groups with English translation by R H Benson (R/B). *Eight songs* op 59: (nos 1-4 and 5-8), with English translation by E M Traquair (R/B); nos 3 and 4 are ' Regenlied ' and ' Nachklang ', each with a similar distinctive phrase that Brahms used later in the finale of his first sonata for violin and piano. *Nine songs* op 63: nos 1-4 with poems by Max von Schenkendorf, and 5-9, which include ' Meine Liebe ist grün ' (Felix Schumann) and the three ' Heimweh ' songs by the north German poet Klaus Groth; with English translation by N Macfarren (Peters).

Songs without opus number

These include ' Mondnacht ' (Eichendorff) (Peters, book II) and ' Regenlied ' (Klaus Groth), op posth, facsimile of the latter by Hermann Stange (DBG). The words are those set by Brahms in his *Nachklang* op 59 no 4, of which, according to O E Deutsch, this posthumous ' Regenlied ' is the first version.

Fünf Ophelia Lieder (*Five Songs of Ophelia*) op posth: from Shakespeare's *Hamlet* in Schlegel and Tieck's translation. By Karl Geiringer, with foreword in German and English (Sch), 1934, and Schönborn Verlag, Vienna, 1960; by Gerd Sievers with English by W J Craig (B&H), Wiesbaden, 1961 (not in CE). Brahms composed these five songs for solo voice without accompaniment (which he added for practical purposes), at the request of an actor friend, Joseph Lewinsky, for performance by his fiancée, Olga Precheisen, when they appeared together in *Hamlet* at the German Opera in Prague, December 22 1873.

Selections

Editions containing representative selections of Brahms's songs with English translations include *Fifty selected songs*, with English translations by Henry G Chapman and introduction by H E Krehbiel (S/C), and *Fifteen favourite songs*, with new translations by A H Fox-Strangways and Steuart Wilson (OUP). An unusual edition of the best known songs is *Brahms Lieder,* arranged for piano solo by Max Reger (s/l). It consists of twenty eight songs in four books, each of seven songs, with the texts added in German and English, the latter by Paul England. The vocal melodic line is indicated clearly throughout.

Folksong settings (all in CE XXVI)

Volks-Kinderlieder, mit hinzugefügter Clavierbegleitung, den Kindern Robert und Clara Schumann gedwidmet (*Children's Folksongs* with added accompaniment, dedicated to the children of Robert and Clara Schumann): first published anonymously in 1858 (R/B) with English translations by M B Whiting (Novello's School Songs); by Florence Hoare (Curwen), and by H S Drinker in DCLM. Also as 'Popular nursery songs' with English translation by E M Traquair (Peters). No 4 is 'Sandmännchen' ('The little dustman'). *Neue Volkslieder*: thirty two in all, of which nos 1-28 are for solo voice and nos 29-32 for four part mixed choir (*see Folksong settings for choir*), by Max Friedlaender from a manuscript belonging to Clara Schumann (DBG). *Deutsche Volkslieder* (forty nine), in seven books, the first six for solo voice and the seventh for soloist and small four part choir *ad lib* (s/l) and in DLCM.

Vocal arrangements

Brahms's great love for Schubert's music led him to arrange some of this composer's songs with orchestral accompaniment. They are *Memnon, An Schwager Kronos* and *Geheimes,* with preface by W H Hadow (OUP) and *Gruppe aus dem Tartarus,* for unison male choir, with preface by O E Deutsch (OUP). More specialised is the arrangement of 'Ellens Zweiter Gesang' (Ellen's second song, from Scott's *Lady of the lake*) ('Huntsman rest, thy chase is done'), for soprano solo, three part women's choir, four horns and two bassoons (DBG and CE XIX).

Orchestral works

Brahms's orchestral works are few in number compared with those in the other categories of his output. All are easily accessible in miniature scores, and most of them are also available in arrangements for piano solo or duet, often made by the composer himself.

Symphonies

All four symphonies are in various miniature scores (Eul), and without editor's name (WPV, Ric, UE), in Hawkes' Pocket Scores (Boosey), and by Albert E Wier in 'The miniature score series' volume 2 (Heffer, Cambridge, printed in USA). The symphonies are also arranged for piano duet, no editor's name (S/C), and by Otto Singer for piano duet and for piano solo (Peters).

First symphony in C minor op 68 (CE I): orchestral score, 'study and conducting format containing piano arrangement' by Anis Fuleihan (Southern).

Second symphony in D major op 73 (CE I).

Third symphony in F major op 90 (CE II), facsimile of the autograph, with various piano pieces (Robert Owen Lehmann Foundation, Washington).

Fourth symphony in E minor op 98 (CE II). All four arranged by Brahms for piano duet and no 4 for two pianos (S/L). No 3 arranged for piano solo by Daniel Gregory Mason (Sch).

Concertos

Piano concerto no 1 in D minor op 15 (CE VI). Miniature score (Eul) and by A E Wier in 'Miniature arrow score' (Longmans, NY), with 'Arrow' system of indicating the melodic and structural outline and calling attention to significant threads in the texture. Folio size with very clear small print. Two piano score by Edwin Hughes (S/C); also arranged by Brahms for piano duet and for two pianos (R/B).

Piano concerto no 2 in B flat op 83 (CE VI). Miniature score (Eul), by Wier (Longmans, NY); no editor (Ric and Boosey); arranged for two pianos by Edwin Hughes (S/C) and by Brahms for two pianos (S/L) and for piano duet (R/B), and with second piano by Emil von Sauer (Augener).

Violin concerto in D op 77 (CE V). Miniature scores (Eul), by Wier (Longmans, NY), by Gordon Jacob (Penguin), no editor (Boosey and Ric). Score with violin part by Maxim Jacobsen (Augener); for violin and piano, with cadenza, by Joseph Joachim (S/L); by Efrem Zimbalist (S/C); by Leopold Auer (Carl Fischer, NY); by Joseph Szigeti (Curci, Milan). Cadenzas for this concerto have also been composed by Oscar Back (Broekmans & Van Poppel, Amsterdam), F Bonavia (Novello), Adolf Busch (B&H), F Busoni (Simrock), F Kreisler (Schott) and many others. One by Donald Tovey, with introductory matter (OUP, London, and Carl Fischer, NY).

Double concerto in A minor op 102: for violin and violoncello (CE V). Miniature scores (Eul) and by Wier (Longmans, NY).

Other orchestral works

Two serenades (CE IV): no 1 in D op 11 for full orchestra. Miniature score (Eul), arranged for piano duet by Brahms (B&H). No 2 in A op 16 for small orchestra. Miniature score (Eul), arranged for piano duet by Brahms (S/L).

Variations on a theme by Haydn (*Chorale St Anthony*) op 56a (CE III). Miniature scores (Eul), no editor (WPV, UE, Boosey, Ric) and by Hubert Foss and Gordon Jacob (Penguin). Arranged for piano solo by Ludwig Stark (L) and without editor's name (S/C). (*See also under Works for two pianos,* as op 56b.)

Academic festival overture op 80 (CE III). Miniature scores (Eul), no editor (Boosey and Ric); 'Study and conducting format containing piano arrangement' by Anis Fuleihan (Southern); arranged for piano duet by Brahms (S/C).

Tragic overture op 81 (CE III). Miniature scores (Eul), no editor (Boosey, Ric, Goodwin & Tabb); arranged by Brahms for piano duet (S/L).

Hungarian dances: nos 1, 3 and 10, orchestrated by Brahms (CE IV) (S/L) (*see also Piano duets*).

Chamber music

Brahms's extensive production of chamber music, which fills four volumes of the CE, comprises two sextets, three quintets (one is the clarinet quintet), and three quartets, all for strings (CE VII), a piano quintet and three piano quartets (CE VIII), three piano trios, a horn trio and a clarinet trio (CE IX), all in miniature score by Altmann (Eul). In addition, seven piano duos (sonatas) and a single movement for violin and piano (CE X).

Collected editions of the works are as follows:

The complete string chamber music of Brahms: originally issued by the Vienna Gesellschaft der Musikfreunde (CE VII), reissued, slightly reduced in size and with an English translation of Hans

Gal's preface (Dover Publishing Company, NY; Constable, London); and *The chamber music of Brahms:* by A E Wier (Miniature arrow scores, Longmans, NY). (*See Piano concerto no 1* for description of these scores.)

Editions of individual works alternative to CE and Eul are given below:

Works for strings (CE VII): *Sextet in B flat* op 18 for two violins, two violas and two cellos, arranged by Brahms for piano duet (S/L); the second movement (variations) arranged by Brahms for piano solo for Clara Schumann (CE XV), and in book II of *Brahms's complete piano works* (Ric); facsimile of the autograph of this version, with other works (Robert Owen Lehmann Foundation, Washington); *Sextet in G* op 36 for two violins, two violas and two cellos, arranged by Brahms for piano duet (S/L); *Quintet in F* op 88 for two violins, two violas and cello, arranged for piano duet by Brahms (S/L). *Quintet in G* op 111 for two violins, two violas and cello, arranged for piano duet by Brahms (S/L). *Quintet in B minor* op 115 for clarinet, two violins, viola and cello. Miniature scores by F J Thurston with analysis (Boosey) and without editor's name (Ric).

Piano quintet and quartets (CE VIII): *Piano quintet in F minor* op 34: score and parts (S/C), miniature score (Ric) (*see also sonata for two pianos* op 34b (S/L)). *Piano quartet in G minor* op 25 arranged for piano duet by Brahms (S/L), orchestrated by Arnold Schoenberg; facsimile of Schoenberg's autograph score (Sch). This extremely effective translation of a classic of chamber music into orchestral terms by a musical revolutionary is an outcome of Schoenberg's admiration for Brahms as a definitely forward looking composer. In his book *Style and idea,* translated by Dika Newlin (Williams & Norgate), Schoenberg devoted a whole chapter (pp 52-101), entitled ' Brahms the progressive ', to a minute and sympathetic analysis of his compositional procedures. It infinitely repays study, and the facsimile score itself is a thing of great beauty. The last movement of this quartet, ' Rondo alla Zingarese ', was arranged for piano solo by Ernst von Dohnányi (Rózsavölgyi, Budapest). *Piano quartet in A major* op 26: score and parts (Sch);

arranged for piano duet by Brahms (S/L). *Piano quartet in C minor* op 60: score and parts (S/C).

String quartets (CE VII): two *String quartets,* op 51 no 1 in C minor, no 2 in A minor. *String quartet in B flat* op 67: all three quartets in miniature score, by Karl Geiringer (WPV), without editor's name (Boosey and Ric). All arranged by Brahms for piano duet (Simrock's Volksausgabe, S/L).

Piano trios (CE IX): *Trio in B* op 8 for violin, cello and piano. It exists in two versions, the original edition 'Erste Fassung' (B&H), which Brahms composed in 1853-4, having been fundamentally revised by him and reissued in 1891 as 'Neue Ausgabe'. It is this later version which is now generally performed. Score by Joseph Adamowski (S/C); arranged for piano duet by Brahms (S/L). *Trio in E flat* op 40 for violin, horn (or cello or viola) and piano, known as the 'Horn trio': miniature score (S/L). *Trio in C major* op 87 for violin, cello and piano: miniature score (S/L). *Trio in C minor* op 101 for violin, cello and piano: score by J Adamowski (Sch) and by Georg Schumann (Augener). *Trio in A minor* op 114 for clarinet (viola), cello and piano: facsimile of the autograph, with commentary on the work by Alfons Ott (Hans Schneider, Tutzing, Bavaria). *Trio in A flat major* op posth for piano, violin and cello: piano score and parts by Ernst Bücken and Karl Hasse (B&H), 1938. Thought to have been composed by Brahms in 1853, the work is considered by O E Deutsch as of doubtful authenticity (not in CE).

Piano duos (CE X): *Sonatensatz (Sonata movement), Scherzo in C major for violin and piano,* op posth. This is the movement that Brahms composed for the sonata written jointly by Schumann, Albert Dietrich and himself in honour of Joseph Joachim in 1853. It was the first publication of the *Deutsche Brahms Gesellschaft* in 1906 (B&H), later reissued as no 6049 of Edition Breitkopf. A more recent edition is by Hans Otto Hiekel (Henle, Munich).

Three sonatas for violin and piano: no 1 in G op 76, no 2 in A op 100, no 3 in D minor op 108; all three by Artur Schnabel and Carl Flesch (Peters); by Franz Kneisel and Harold Bauer (S/C); by H O Hiekel (Henle, Munich); by Maxim Jacobsen (Augener); and in LPS no 6 (UE).

Two sonatas for cello and piano: no 1 in E minor op 38 by Hans Münch-Holland (Henle); by Edwin Hughes and Cornelius van Vliet (Augener); and in LPS no 7 (UE); arranged for viola and piano by Lionel Tertis (Augener). No 2 in F major op 99 by H Münch-Holland (Henle); and by J Klengel (Augener); and in LPS no 6 (UE).

Two sonatas for clarinet (viola or violin) and piano op 120: no 1 in F minor, no 2 in E flat major. Both arranged for violin and piano by Brahms (S/L); this latter version also by Oswald Jonas with facsimiles, scores and parts (S/L); arranged for viola by Lionel Tertis (Augener); original version for clarinet and piano by Heinrich Bading (Peters); for violin and piano by Carl Herrmann (Peters). Each sonata separately, (clarinet edition) (Boosey); and jointly with the two cello sonatas in LPS no 7 (UE).

Piano music
Brahms had powerful incentives to composing music for piano. He was himself a concert pianist and among his circle of friends were a number of fine performers, such as Clara Schumann, Carl Tausig, Ignaz Brüll and Hans von Bülow, ready and eager to play his works, whether for solo or duet. As a teacher, too, he was led to compose studies of various types and grades of difficulty. The whole of the piano music listed here (with two exceptions marked *) is printed in CE XI-XV.

Works for two pianos (CE XI): *Sonata in F minor* op 34b after the piano quintet op 34 (R/B and Hinrichsen). Arranged for piano duet by Theodor Kirchner at Brahms's suggestion (S/L). *Variations on a theme by Haydn* op 56b (Brahms's own alternative version of the better known orchestral work of the same title, op 56a); by Edwin Hughes (S/C), no editor (Hinrichsen) and in LPS no 19 (UE).

Works for piano duet (CE XII): *Variations on a theme in E flat by Schumann* op 23 facsimile of the autograph, with other works (Robert Owen Lehmann Foundation, Washington); no editor (Peters); arranged for two pianos by Th Kirchner (S/L). *Waltzes* op 39 (Peters); arranged for two pianos by Edwin Hughes (S/C); transcribed for orchestra (with finale) by Reynaldo Hahn (Heugel, Paris). No 8 arranged for guitar by Andrés Segovia (Schott) (*see also under Piano solos*) *Liebeslieder Waltzer* op 52a and *Neue*

Liebeslieder Waltzer op 65a, arranged by Brahms for piano duet without the vocal parts (s/L) (*see also under Vocal quartets*). *Hungarian dances* (21) in four books (without opus number), by W Scharfenberg (s/c), and by Otto Singer (Peters). Nos 1-10 arranged for piano solo by Brahms (CE XV), (s/L), in LPS no 157 (UE); and nos 11-21 by T Kirchner (s/L). All 21 in book II of *Complete piano works* (Ric). Arranged for violin and piano by J Joachim (s/L); the same revised by Leopold Auer (s/c); arranged for cello and piano by Alfredo Piatti (s/L). Nos 1, 3 and 10 arranged for orchestra by Brahms (CE IV) and (s/L). A vocal offshoot: *Zigeunerlied* (*Gipsy Song*), arranged by Pauline Viardot as a duet for two women's voices after one of Brahms's Hungarian dances, with German words by Frau Malybrok-Stieler and English translation by Mrs J P Morgan (s/L and Sch) (not in CE).

Brahms's first piano duets had been composed to fulfil a commission from the Hamburg publisher A Cranz, who engaged a number of musicians to make elaborate transcriptions of popular airs for printing under the composite name of ' G W Marks '. One of Brahms's early efforts in this medium has survived for documentation: *Souvenir de la Russie** : transcriptions en forme de fantaisies sur des airs russes et bohémiens, composées pour le piano à quatre mains par G W Marks, op 151 (Cranz, Hamburg) *c*1852. Among the six airs included is the Russian national anthem with varieties of florid figuration in both parts which are little typical of Brahms's own style of composition. Another production of this type, for piano *solo*, was a *Collection de potpourris et fantaisies des meilleurs opéras, pour piano**, six numbers, including extracts from operas by Wagner, Meyerbeer, Verdi and Bellini. This was the first of Brahms's works for piano solo to see the light of print, in *c*1852.

Works for piano solo

The whole of the music for piano solo fills three volumes of the CE. Volume XIII is devoted to the sonatas and sets of variations, volume XIV to smaller works in nine opus groups and volume XV to studies, arrangements and little known pieces such as cadenzas to concertos by other composers. In other collected editions the works are arranged in differing succession: either chronologically according to opus number, or in specific categories or irregular sequence.

The three modern practical editions which follow the text of the CE most closely are Henle, Ricordi and Lea Pocket Scores. The first of these, by Walter Georgii, claims to be based on the composer's copies and autographs, and incorporates his scanty pedal markings throughout. Unfortunately, the edition is still incomplete, omitting the variations and the items without opus number. Book I (1952) gives all the groups of pieces from op 76-119, and book II (1956) the three sonatas, the scherzo op 4 and the ballades op 10.

Slightly more recent and infinitely more complete is Brahms: *opere complete per pianoforte*, in two books (Ric), 1957, without an editor's name but described as ' in conformity with the originals '. Book I contains the sonatas, the scherzo, all the sets of variations, the waltzes (in two versions) and the eight pieces of op 76; book II the rhapsodies, the four groups of intermezzi and capricci op 116-119, and all the works without opus number, which include the Hungarian dances, several studies, and cadenzas for concertos by Bach, Mozart and Beethoven. There is only one omission: the musically unimportant but technically useful books of *51 Uebungen* (keyboard exercises). They are, however, issued separately by the same publisher.

The more recent Lea Pocket Scores edition (UE) in four books is far from complete as yet, but has the merit of being actually reprinted (in smaller format) from the CE. No 19 gives the five sets of variations (and the ' Haydn ' variations for two pianos); no 57 the three sonatas; no 66 all the groups of single pieces op 76, 79 and 116-119; no 157 (1968) the four ballades, scherzo, waltzes, the first ten of the Hungarian dances and Brahms's arrangement for left hand of Bach's chaconne in D minor for solo violin.

The following list of all the individual works includes other editions beyond those already mentioned, and indicates which single items from collected editions are also available separately.

Works with opus numbers: Three sonatas, op 1 in C, op 2 in F sharp minor, op 5 in F minor (CE XIII), all three sonatas by A Whiting (s/c) no 3 also by Harold Bauer with extensive notes and reasoned preface comparing other editions and aiming at ' clearing

91

away certain ambiguities of the original ' (s/c), 1935. *Scherzo in E flat minor* op 4 (CE XIV), by Evelyn Howard-Jones (Ric), 1908. *Four ballades* op 10 (CE XIV), no 1 in D minor (after the Scottish ballad ' Edward '), no 2 in D major, no 3 in B minor (intermezzo), no 4 in B major (s/c). *Variations on a theme in F sharp minor by Schumann,* op 9 (CE XIII), by Isidore Philipp (Durand, Paris), and by Montani (Ric). *Variations on an original theme* op 21 no 1 and *Variations on a Hungarian song* op 21 no 2 (CE XIII) (Ric) *Variations on a theme by Handel, Studies for piano* op 24 (CE XIII), facsimile of the autograph, with other works (Robert Owen Lehmann Foundation, Washington); by Montani (Ric); arranged for piano duet by Th Kirchner (B&H), orchestrated by Edmund Rubbra (UE) 1938. *Variations on a theme by Paganini, Studies for piano* op 35 (CE XIII), in two books, by Edwin Hughes (s/c), by Montani (Ric) and by Emil Sauer (Peters).

Waltzes op 39 (CE XIV), arranged by Brahms for piano solo from the original version for piano duet, with pedalling and fingering by A Whiting (s/c). The simplified edition made by Brahms himself is printed in Ric Book II and is issued separately by Henle, but is not included in LPS.

Eight capricci and intermezzi op 76 (CE XIV), by A Whiting (s/c); no 2 in B minor, version by I Philipp (Sch) and for two pianos, four hands, by Henry Geehl (Ashdown). *Two rhapsodies* op 79 no 1 in B minor, no 2 in G minor (CE XIV), by Gebhard (s/c) and by Montani (Ric). *Fantasies* op 116 (three capricci and four intermezzi) (CE IV), by Carl Deis (s/c) and by W Georgii (Henle). *Three intermezzi* op 117 (CE XIV), by C Deis (s/c), by W Georgii (Henle and Ric). *Six pieces* op 118 (four intermezzi, ballade in G minor and romance in F major) (CE XIV), by C Deis (s/c) and by W Georgii (Henle). *Four pieces* op 119 (three intermezzi and rhapsody in E flat (CE XIV)) by C Deis (s/c), by W Georgii (Henle) and by R Locatelli (Ric).

Works without opus numbers (all in CE XV): *Hungarian dances,* nos 1-10 arranged by Brahms from the originals for duet; by Scharfenberg (s/c) and by W Georgii (Henle). *Two sarabandes* and *Two gigues,* with introduction by Kurt Hermann (Hinrichsen); the sarabandes *only,* in facsimile with foreword by Max Friedlaender (DBG). *Theme and variations in D minor* from the string sextet in G op 18, arranged by Brahms for Clara Schumann; by Montani (Ric). *Fifty one Uebungen* (exercises), by Pozzoli (Ric), and no editor (S/C).

Brahms's arrangements of other composers' works (all in CE XV).

Five studies: F Chopin *Study in F minor* op 25 no 2 (right hand part arranged in sixths), Weber *Rondo* (*moto perpetuo*) from *Sonata in C* (right hand part transferred to left hand), Bach *Presto in G major for solo violin* (with counterpoint added by Brahms), in two versions (the second with the right hand and left hand parts reversed), Bach *Chaconne in D minor for solo violin* (arranged for the left hand alone). All five studies in Ric book II; by E Sauer (Peters), and each separately (B&H). Schubert *Impromptu in E flat* op 90 no 2 (the right hand and left hand parts interchanged) op posth (Ric Book II). Gluck *Gavotte in A* from the opera *Iphigenia in Aulis*, arranged by Brahms from memory; by E Sauer (Peters) and in Ric, book II.

Cadenzas (all in CE XV and in Ricordi book II)
Two to Beethoven *Concerto in G* op 78 (also in DBG)
One to Beethoven *Concerto in C minor* op 37
One to Bach *Concerto in D minor*
One to Mozart *Concerto in G major* K453
One to Mozart *Concerto in D minor,* K466 (jointly with Clara Schumann)
One to Mozart *Concerto in C minor,* K491.

Works for organ (all in CE XVI)

Two preludes and fugues, no 1 in A minor, no 2 in G minor op posth. *Fugue in A flat minor* without opus number, by John E West (Novello), no editor (L). *Chorale prelude and fugue in A minor* (' O Traurigkeit, O Herzeleid ') without opus number (DBG), and by J E West (Novello). *Eleven choral preludes* op 122 in two books, by E Mandyczewski (Simrock), 1902; by J E West (Novello); arranged for piano solo by Paul Juon (S/L); nos 4, 5 and 8-11 arranged for piano by F Busoni (S/L). All eleven orchestrated by Virgil Thompson (Boosey). No 11, ' O Welt ich muss dich lassen ' (Brahms's very last composition), facsimile in CE XVI. All these items together in *Brahms: complete organ works,* with a foreword and facsimiles of three of the choral preludes, by W E Buszin and P G Bunjes, in two books (Peters edition nos 6333a and 6333b) and a supplementary book (no 6333c) containing alternative versions of op 122 nos 2 and 5-7 with addition of another manual or the pedal.

Brahms as editor

In addition to the elaborating of instrumental works by other composers (*eg* the five studies, etc), which became essentially Brahmsian in the process, Brahms made straightforward arrangements of a number of items of choral, solo vocal, and orchestral music for various publishers, sometimes anonymously. Among such re-arrangements were Schubert's *Mass in E flat* for piano solo (R/B), Schumann's *Piano quartet in E flat* op 47 for piano duet (Fürstner, Berlin), eleven of Schubert's *Ländler* for piano duet, from the original for piano solo (Schott), etc. He wrote accompaniments from figured basses to *Thirteen duets* and *Two trios* by Handel for the German Handel Society, and to two *Sonatas for violin and clavier* by C P E Bach (R/B). With Friedrich Chrysander he edited the keyboard music of François Couperin (Augener), and was a member of the several editorial boards concerned with bringing out the complete works of Mozart, Schubert, Chopin and Schumann. It was Brahms who discovered the five extra variations of the last-named composer's *Études symphoniques* and saw to their publication.

Brahms the contrapuntist

Oktaven und Quinten (aus dem Nachlass herausgegeben und erläutert von Heinrich Schenker) (UE, no 10508), 1933: a facsimile of a Brahms autograph comprising music examples demonstrating the occurrence of octaves and fifths in the part writing of early and later composers, transcribed by Brahms in connexion with his own studies in counterpoint. The editor gives full descriptions and explanations of the text for all who cannot decipher Brahms's old German handwriting (*Fraktur*). The quotations drawn from Gabrieli, Bach, Cherubini and others show how deeply interested Brahms was in studying earlier contrapuntal writing. The editing

94

of the facsimile was the last work undertaken by H Schenker (1867-1935), an Austrian-Polish musicologist who had known Brahms, and whose own individual method of musical analysis depended ideally upon the consultation of the sketches and autographs of works under survey.

Selected recordings of Brahms's music

COMPILED BY BRIAN REDFERN

Like the earlier discographies of Beethoven and Mozart in this series, this one is a personal choice. But as Brahms wrote fewer compositions than the other composers, it has been possible to include more recordings of individual works when available. Except for the items listed under *Lieder,* where a direct comparison between such varied recitals was impossible, the recordings of each work are listed in order of preference. I have not included a poor recording, although a hi-fi enthusiast might not like the two included for historical interest. However, I have given at least one record for each item by Brahms in the current catalogue, so that the reader may become acquainted with all Brahms's music on record if he wishes. When many records are listed under one composition, at least the first three are of outstanding quality. The remainder of the items are considered excellent.

When a recording included in the list has been deleted, it may be possible to borrow it from one of the many public gramophone libraries in both the United Kingdom and the United States. Quite often a full-price recording reappears on a cheaper label after its deletion at the higher price.

The order under each musical form can be quickly seen, except in the case of *Lieder* recordings, which are listed alphabetically by artist. In order to avoid consultation of secondary lists and indexes I have tried to make the abbreviations of orchestral and other names intelligible on their own. Performers are cited as appropriate in the order: soloists, choir, orchestra, conductor.

96

Any second catalogue number given is American. If there is no second number the recordings may not be available in America except by import. American readers are referred to the excellent *Schwann* catalogue for prices and for a complete listing of American recordings, which include many only available in the United States, and which I have therefore not been able to hear. For British issues I have indicated the cheaper labels as follows * £1 to £2; † under £1.

Vocal music

CHORAL

Ein Deutsches Requiem op 45:

Schwarzkopf, Fischer-Dieskau; Phil Chorus & Orch; Klemperer. SAXS 2430, SAX 2431 (3 sides); Angel S 3624 (2 recs).

Janowitz, Waechter; Wiener Singverein; Berlin Phil; Karajan. *With* St Anthony variations. SLPM 138928/9; DGG 138928/9.

Caballé, Milnes; New England Conservatory Chorus; Boston Sym; Leinsdorf. *With* Vier ernste Gesänge. SB 6825/1-2 (2 recs); LSC 7054 (2 recs).

Lipp, Crass; Wiener Singverein; Vienna Sym; Sawallisch. *With* Rhapsody for alto, Schicksalslied. †SFL 14057-8.

Grümmer, Fischer-Dieskau; St Hedwig's Cathedral Choir; Berlin Phil; Kempe. *With* Bruckner. Te Deum. *XLP 30073-4.

Nänie op 82:

New Phil Chorus & Orch; Pitz. *Concert.* ASD 2325; Angel S 36428.

Rhapsody for alto, male chorus & orchestra op 53:

Ludwig; Phil Chorus & Orch; Klemperer. *Concert.* ASD 2391; Angel S 35923.

Ferrier; London Phil Choir & Orch; Krauss. *Recital of Brahms's Lieder.* *ACL 306; London 5098.

Heynis; Wiener Singverein; Vienna Sym; Sawallisch. *With* Ein Deutsches Requiem, Schicksalslied. †SFL 14057-8.

Moreira; Innsbruck Sym Chorus & Orch; Wagner. *Concert.* †TV 34281 S; Turnabout 34281.

Rinaldo, cantata for tenor, male chorus & orchestra op 50:

97

King; Ambrosian Chorus; New Phil; Abbado. *With* Schicksalslied. SXL 6386; London 26106.

Schicksalslied for chorus & orchestra op 54:
Ambrosian singers; New Phil; Abbado. *With* Rinaldo. SXL
6386; London 26106.

Wiener Singverein; Vienna Sym; Sawallisch. *With* Ein deutsches
Requiem, Rhapsody for alto. †SFL 14057-8.

*Choral songs (Abendständchen op 42 no 1, Von alten Liebesliedern
op 62 no 2, Waldesnacht op 62 no 3, Dein Herzlein mild op 62 no
4, Herzgedanken op 62 no 5, O süsser Mai op 93a no 3, Nachtwache
op 104 no 2; Folksongs—Die Wollust in den Maien. In stiller Nacht):*
Bremen Camerata Vocale, Leipzig University Choir. *H 71081;
Nonesuch 71081.

*Motets (Es ist das Heil uns kommen her op 29 no 1, Geistliches
Lied op 30, Warum ist das Licht gegeben op 74 no 1, O Heiland
reiss die Himmel auf op 74 no 2, Ich aber bin elend op 110 no 1,
Ach, arme Welt op 110 no 2, Wenn wir in höchsten Nöten sein op
110 no 3):*
New English Singers; Preston (organ). *With* Chorale-preludes.
ZRG 571; ZRG 571.

FOLK SONG SETTINGS
Deutsche Volkslieder:
Schwarzkopf, Fischer-Dieskau; Moore. SAN 163-4; Angel S 3675
(2 recs).

LIEDER
The variety of songs recorded is so great that it is impossible to
make comparisons. I have therefore listed them alphabetically by
artist and have also indicated the range of voice.
*Von ewiger Liebe op 43 no 1, Die Mainacht op 43 no 2, Die Nachti-
gall op 97 no 1, Das Mädchen spricht op 107 no 3:*
Baker (mezzo-soprano); Isepp. *Recital.* †STXID 5277.
*O liebliche Wangen op 47 no 4, Sommerabend op 85 no 1, Monden-
schein op 85 no 2, Feldeinsamkeit op 86 no 2, Auf dem Kirchhofe
op 105 no 4:*

98

Bumbry (contralto); Hokanson. *Recital.* ASD 2317; Angel S 36454.

Botschaft op 47 no 1, Gestillte Sehnsucht op 91 no 1, Geistliches Wiegenlied op 91 no 2, Sapphische Ode op 94 no 4, Vier ernste Gesänge op 121:

Ferrier (contralto); Gilbert (viola); Spurr. *With* Rhapsody for alto. *ACL 306; London 5098 (not op 121).

Herbstgefühl op 48 no 7, Abenddämmerung op 49 no 5, Auf dem See op 59 no 2, Nachklang op 59 no 4, O wüsst ich doch op 63 no 8, Alte Liebe op 72 no 1, Verzagen op 72 no 4, Frühlingslied op 85 no 5, Feldeinsamkeit op 86 no 2, Mit vierzig Jahren op 94 no 1, Steig auf, geliebter Schatten op 94 no 2, Mein Herz ist schwer op 94 no 3, Kein Haus, Kein Heimat op 94 no 5, Auf dem Kirchhofe op 105 no 4, Regenlied op posth:

Fischer-Dieskau (baritone); Demus. SLPM 138011; DGG 138011.

Die Mainacht op 43 no 2, Sonntag op 47 no 3, Am Sonntag Morgen op 49 no 1, Blinde Kuh op 58 no 1, Dein blaues Auge op 59 no 8, Vier ernste Gesänge op 121, Folksongs—Mir ist ein schöns brauns Maidelein, Da unten im Tale:

Foster (bass-baritone); Schmidt. *GSGC 14091.

Wie rafft ich mich auf op 32 no 1, Minnelied op 71 no 5, Schön war op 95 no 7, Es schauen die Blumen alle op 96 no 3:

Laubenthal (tenor); Werba. *Recital.* †642101.

Gestillte Sehnsucht op 91 no 1, Geistliches Wiegenlied op 91 no 2:

Ludwig (mezzo-soprano); Downes (viola); Parsons. *Recital.* SAX 5274; Angel S 36352.

Vier ernste Gesänge op 121:

Milnes (baritone); Leinsdorf. *With* Ein deutsches Requiem. SB 6825/1-2 (2 recs); LSC 7054 (2 recs).

Sonntag op 47 no 3, O liebliche Wangen op 47 no 4, Es liebt sich so lieblich op 71 no 1, Alte Liebe op 72 no 1, Verzagen op 72 no 4, Sapphische Ode op 94 no 4, Auf dem Kirchhofe op 105 no 4:

Souzay (baritone); Baldwin. *With* Beethoven Lieder. SAL 3422; PHC 3 019 (3 recs). *Recital.*

Magelone romances op 33:

Stämpfli (bass); Galling. †TV 34176 S; Turnabout 34176.

Wiegenlied op 49 no 4, Geheimnis op 71 no 3, Vergebliches Ständ-

chen op 84 no 4, Auf dem Schiffe op 97 no 2, Trennung op 97 no 6, Ständchen op 106 no 1, Das Mädchen spricht op 107 no 3, Mädchen- lied op 107 no 5:

Streich (soprano); Weissenborn. *Recital.* SLPM 138716.

Von ewiger Liebe op 43 no 1, O kühler Wald op 72 no 3, Der Kranz op 84 no 2, Therese op 86 no 1, Komm bald op 97 no 5:

Wolf (soprano); Isepp. *Recital.* *UNS 205.

Orchestral music

SYMPHONIES

These are among the most recorded works in the repertoire and interpretations differ widely. Those who want great power should turn to Klemperer for the whole set, but only his no 4 is included here. For the romantic Viennese approach either Walter or Barbi- rolli should be chosen. Karajan offers for me the most compelling interpretations of all four symphonies, but as the most faithful to Brahms's intentions I would recommend Cantelli, Kempe, Kertesz, Monteux and Boult where they are listed below.

1 op 68 C minor:

Berlin Phil; Karajan.   SLPM 138924;   DGG 138924.

Phil; Cantelli.   *XLP 30023.

Berlin Phil; Kempe.   †MFP 2012.

Vienna Phil; Barbirolli.   ASD 2401.

Columbia Sym; Walter.   SBRG 72088;   MS 6389.

London Phil; Boult.   †MAL 555;   Stereo Fidelity 14000.

2 op 73 D major:

Vienna Phil; Kertesz.   SXL 6172;   London 6435.

Vienna Phil; Monteux.   *VIC 1055;   Philips S 9123.

Berlin Phil; Karajan.   SLPM 138925;   DGG 138925.

Vienna Phil; Barbirolli. *With* Tragic overture.   ASD 2421.

Royal Phil; Beecham. *With* Academic festival overture.   *HQS 1143;   Seraphim S 60083.

Berlin Phil; Böhm.   †89595.

3 op 90 F major:

Vienna Phil; Barbirolli. *With* St Anthony variations.   ASD 2432.

Phil; Cantelli. *With* Schumann Sym 4.   *XLP 30030.

Berlin Phil; Karajan. *With St Anthony variations.* SLPM 138926; DGG 138926.

Berlin Phil; Kempe. *With* Tragic overture. *SXLP 30100.

Columbia Sym; Walter. SBRG 72090; MS 6174 (*With* St Antony variations).

New York Phil; Bernstein. *With* Academic festival overture. SBRG 72524; MS 6909.

4 op 98 E minor:

Berlin Phil; Karajan. SLPM 138927; DGG 138927.

Phil; Klemperer. SAX 2350; Angel S 35546.

Royal Phil; Kempe. *ST 932.

Columbia Sym; Walter. SBRG 72091; MS 6113.

Hallé Orch; Barbirolli. *GSGC 14037.

Lamoureux Orch; Markevich. *With* Beethoven. Namensfeier overture. †89694.

CONCERTOS

Again the choice for the piano concertos and the violin concerto is very wide. In each case the first recording listed is a clear winner for me. After that the order is less certain.

Piano concerto no 1 op 15 D minor:

Serkin; Cleveland Orch; Szell. SBRG 72718; MS 7143.

Barenboim; New Phil; Barbirolli. ASD 2353; Angel S 36463.

Curzon; Amsterdam Concertgebouw Orch; Van Beinum. *ACL 227.

Arrau; Phil; Giulini. SAX 2387.

Graffman; Boston Sym; Munch. *VICS 1109; VICS 1109.

Piano concerto no 2 op 83 B flat major:

Backhaus; Vienna Phil; Böhm. SXL 6322; London 6550.

Ashkenazy; London Sym; Mehta. SXL 6309; London 6539.

Solomon; Phil; Dobrowen. *XLP 30093.

Gilels; Chicago Sym; Reiner. *VICS 1026; VICS 1026.

Serkin; Cleveland Orch; Szell. SBRG 72557; MS 6967.

Barenboim; New Phil; Barbirolli. ASD 2413; Angel S 36526.

Watts; New York Phil; Bernstein SBRG 72688; MS 7134.

E Fischer; Berlin Phil; Furtwängler. *Historical interest.* UNI 102; Turnabout 4342.

4*

Violin concerto op 77 D major:
Menuhin; Berlin Phil; Kempe. ASD 264.
Francescatti; New York Phil; Bernstein. *CBS 61123; MS 6471.
D Oistrakh; French Nat Radio Orch; Klemperer. SAX 2411; Angel S 35836.
Kogan; Phil; Kondrashin. *SXLP 30063; Seraphim S 60059.
Grumiaux; Amsterdam Concertgebouw Orch; Van Beinum. *With* Bruch. Violin concerto. SAL 3526.
D Oistrakh; Cleveland Orch; Szell. *With* Double concerto *SLS 786/1-2 (2 recs not available separately). Angel S 36033 (op 77 only).
Gimpel; Berlin Sym; Gruber. *With* Mendelssohn. Violin concerto. †MAL 809.
Kreisler; London Phil; Barbirolli. *Historical interest.* *SH 115.
Double concerto for violin & cello op 102 A minor:
D Oistrakh; Rostropovich; Cleveland Orch; Szell. *With* Violin concerto. *SLS 786/1-2 (2 recs not available separately). Angel S 36032 (op 102 only).
D Oistrakh; Fournier; Phil; Galliera. *With* Tragic overture. SAX 2264; Angel S 35353.
Stern; Rose; Philadelphia Orch; Ormandy. *With* Variations on a theme by Handel. SBRG 72295; MS 7251 (*With* Mozart. Sinfonia concertante K364) or D2S 720 (2 recs *With* piano trio 2 & Beethoven. Triple concerto).
Suk; Navarra; Czech Phil; Ančerl. *With* Tragic overture. *SUAST 50573; Parlophone S 601 (op 102 only).

OTHER ORCHESTRAL MUSIC
Academic festival overture op 80:
Berlin Phil; Abbado.*With* Serenade no 2. SLPM 139371; DGG 139371.
New York Phil; Bernstein. *With* Sym 3. SBRG 72524.
Royal Phil; Beecham. *With* Sym 2. *HQS 1143; Seraphim S 60083.

Amsterdam Concertgebouw Orch; Van Beinum. *With* St Anthony variations and Tragic overture. †ECS 520.

Hungarian dances nos 1, 5, 6, 7, 12, 13, 19, 21:
Vienna Phil; Reiner. *With* Dvořák. Slavonic dances nos 1, 3, 8, 9, 10. *SDD 123; STS 15009.

St Anthony variations op 56 A:
Phil; Giulini. *With* Schubert. Sym 8. SAX 2424.
Vienna Phil; Barbirolli. *With* Sym 3. ASD 2432.
Berlin Phil; Karajan. *With* Ein Deutsches Requiem. SLPM 138928/9 DGG 138928/9.
Berlin Phil; Karajan. *With* Sym 3. SLPM 138926; DGG 138926.
Amsterdam Concertgebouw Orch; Van Beinum. *With* Academic festival overture & Tragic overture. †ECS 520.

Serenade no 1 op 11 D major:
London Sym; Kertesz. SXL 6340; London 6567.

Serenade no 2 op 16 A major:
London Sym; Kertesz. *With* Dvořák. Serenade for wind. SXL 6368.
Berlin Phil; Abbado. *With* Academic festival overture. SLPM 139371; DGG 139371.
Dresden Phil; Bongartz. *With* Dvořák. Serenade for strings. *DGG 135038.

Tragic overture op 81:
Phil; Galliera. *With* Double concerto. SAX 2264; Angel S 35353.
Vienna Phil; Barbirolli. *With* Sym 2. ASD 2421.
Berlin Phil; Kempe. *With* Sym 3. *SXLP 30100.
Czech Phil; Ančerl. *With* Double concerto. *SUAST 50573.
Amsterdam Concertgebouw Orch; Van Beinum. *With* Academic festival overture & St Anthony variations. †ECS 520.

Variations on a theme by Haydn:
See St Anthony variations.

Chamber music
SEXTETS
String sextet no 1 op 18 B flat major:
Members of Berlin Phil octet. SAL 3599; Philips 9050.

Amadeus Quartet; Aronowitz (viola); Pleeth (cello). SLPM 139353; DGG 139353.

String sextet no 2 op 36 G major:
Members of Berlin Phil Octet. SAL 3763.

QUINTETS

Clarinet quintet op 115 B minor:
De Peyer; Melos Ensemble. *With* Reger. Clarinet quintet—2nd movement. ASD 620; Angel S 36280.

Boskovsky; Members of Vienna Octet. *With* Wagner(?). Adagio. SXL 2297; London 6234.

Leister; Amadeus Quartet. SLPM 139354; DGG 139354.

Riha; Smetana Quartet. *With* Mozart. Duo K 423. *SUAST 50677.

Brymer; Prometheus Ensemble. TPLS 13004.

Piano quintet op 34 F minor:
Serkin; Budapest Quartet. SBRG 72273; MS 6631.

Rubinstein; Guarneri Quartet. SB 6737; LSC 2971.

Eschenbach; Amadeus Quartet. SLPM 139397; DGG 139397.

See also Sonata for two pianos p 107.

String quintet no 1 op 88 F major, no 2 op 111 G major:
Amadeus Quartet; Aronowitz (viola). SLPM 139430; DGG 139430.

QUARTETS

Piano quartet no 1 op 25 G minor:
Szolchàny; Hungarian Quartet. †TV 34037 S; Turnabout 34037.

Piano quartet no 1 op 25 G minor (orchestrated by Schoenberg):
Chicago Sym; Craft. *Concert of Schoenberg's music.* SBRG 72546-7; MS 752 (2 recs).

Piano quartet no 2 op 26 A minor:
Demus; Amadeus Quartet. SLPM 139439.

Piano quartet no 3 op 60 C minor:
Trio Santoliquido; Guiranna (viola). *With* Dvořák. Trio no 4. SLPM 138966.

String quartet no 1 op 51 no 1 C minor:

Amadeus Quartet. *With* Quartet 2.　SLPM 138114.

Weller Quartet. *With* Quartet 2.　SXL 6151.

Italian Quartet. *With* Schumann. Quartet 1.　SAL 3639;　Philips 900187.

Bartók Quartet. *With* Quartet 2.　*SLPX 1283.

String quartet no 2 op 51 no 2 A minor:

Amadeus Quartet. *With* Quartet 1.　SLPM 138114.

Weller Quartet. *With* Quartet 1.　SXL 6151.

Tatrai Quartet. *With* Mendelssohn. Quartet 4.　†89531.

Bartók Quartet. *With* Quartet 2.　*SLPX 1283.

String quartet no 3 op 67 B flat major:

Amadeus Quartet. *With* Dvořák. Quartet 6.　SLPM 138126; DGG 138126.

Budapest Quartet. *With* Schumann. Piano quintet. SBRG 72429; M2S 734 (2 recs 3 quartets. *With* Schumann. Piano quintet).

TRIOS

Clarinet trio op 114 A minor:

Leister (clarinet); Donderer (cello); Eschenbach (piano). *With* Horn trio.　SLPM 139398;　DGG 139398.

D Glazer (clarinet); Soyer (cello); F Glazer (piano). *With* Beethoven. Clarinet trio.　†TV 34108 S;　Turnabout 34108.

Horn trio op 40 E flat major:

Tuckwell (horn); Perlman (violin); Ashkenazy (piano). *With* Franck. Violin sonata.　SXL 6408;　London 6628.

Melos Ensemble. *Recital.*　SOL 314.

Seifert (horn); Drolc (violin); Eschenbach (piano). *With* clarinet trio.　SLPM 139398;　DGG 139398.

Civil (horn); Y Menuhin (violin); H Menuhin (piano). *With* Piano trio 2.　ASD 2354;　Angel S 36472.

Piano trio no 1 op 8 B major:

Beaux Arts Trio. *With* Trio 2.　SAL 3627;　S PHC 2013 (2 recs trios complete).

Katchen (piano); Suk (violin); Starker (cello). *With* Trio 3.　SXL 6387;　London 6611.

Istomin (piano); Stern (violin); Rose (cello). *With* Trios 2 & 3. SBRG 72596-7; M2S 760.

Piano trio no 2 op 87 C major:

Beaux Arts Trio. *With* Trio 1. SAL 3627; S PHC 2 013 (2 recs trios complete).

Trio di Trieste. *With* Trio 3. SLPM 139182.

Oromonte Trio. *With* Haydn. Piano trio 4 (Hob XV 28). TPLS 13018.

Istomin (piano); Stern (violin); Rose (cello). *With* Trios 1 & 3. SBRG 72596-7; M2S 760.

H Menuhin (piano); Y Menuhin (violin); Gendron (cello). *With* Horn trio. ASD 2354; Angel S 36472.

Piano trio 3 op 101 C minor:

Beaux Arts Trio. *With* Trio op posth A major. SAL 3628; S PHC 2 013 (2 recs trios complete).

Suk Trio. *With* Mendelssohn. Piano trio 1. *SUAST 50815.

Trio di Trieste. *With* Trio 2. SLPM 139182.

Katchen (piano); Suk (violin); Starker (cello). *With* Trio 1. SXL 6387; London 6611.

Istomin (piano); Stern (violin); Rose (cello). *With* Trios 1 & 2. SBRG 72596-7; M2S 760.

Piano trio op posth A major:

Beaux Arts Trio. *With* Trio 3. SAL 3628; S PHC 2 013 (2 recs. Trios complete).

DUOS

Clarinet sonatas no 1 op 120 no 1 F minor, no 2 op 120 no 2 E flat major:

De Peyer (clarinet); Barenboim (piano). ASD 2362.

Violin sonatas no 1 op 78 G major, no 2 op 100 A major, no 3 op 108 D minor:

Suk (violin); Katchen (piano). SXL 6321; London 6549.

Kulenkampff (violin); Solti (piano). *ACL 250.

Violin sonata no 1 op 78 G major:

Röhn (violin); Bergemann (piano). *Recital.* †642103.

Violin sonata no 3 op 108 D minor:

Szigeti (violin); Petri (Piano). *Recital.* *HQM 1127.

Cello sonatas no 1 op 38 E minor, no 2 op 99 F major:
Du Pré (cello); Barenboim (piano). ASD 2436; Angel S 36544.
Fournier (cello); Firkusny (piano). SLPM 139119; DGG 139119.

Piano music
This has been recorded complete by Katchen. Details of this very fine set will be found below under the individual compositions. Occasionally an alternative version is preferred, but anyone wanting one artist's view would find Katchen's interpretation very worthwhile.

PIANO DUETS
Sonata for two pianos op 34 F minor:
Eden, Tamir. *With* Saint-Saens. Variations on a theme by Beethoven. SXL 6303; London 6533.
See also Piano quintet p 104.
Hungarian dances for piano duet nos 1-21 (ie complete):
W Klien; B Klien. †TV 34068 S; Turnabout 34068.
Hungarian dances for solo piano nos 1-10, for piano duet nos 11-21:
Katchen (1-10); Katchen, Marty (11-21). SXL 6217; London 6473.
Hungarian dances for piano duet nos 1-10:
Eden, Tamir. *With* Dvořák. Slavonic dances op 46 for piano duet. SXL 6389; London 6614.
Waltzes op 39:
W Klien, B Klien. *Recital.* †TV 34041 S; Turnabout 34041.
See also Piano solo p 110.

PIANO SOLO
Ballades op 10:
Katchen. *With* Rhapsodies op 79, Waltzes op 39. SXL 6160; London 6444.
8 Piano pieces (Capricci & intermezzi) op 76:
Katchen. *With* Piano pieces op 116. SXL 6118; London 6396.
7 Piano pieces (Fantasias: capricci & intermezzi) op 116:
Katchen. *With* Piano pieces op 76. SXL 6118; London 6396.

7 Piano pieces op 116 nos 1-3 only:
Vazsonyi. *With* piano pieces op 119, Variations on an original theme op 21 no 1. TPLS 13016.
3 Piano pieces (Intermezzi) op 117:
Bishop. *With* Piano pieces op 119, Variations on a theme by Handel op 24. SAL 3758; Philips 3758.
Kempff. *With* Piano pieces op 118, op 119. SLPM 138903; DGG 138903.
Katchen. *With* Piano pieces op 118, op 119. SXL 6105; London 6404.
3 Piano pieces op 117 no 1 only:
Curzon. *With* Intermezzo op 119 no 3, Sonata 3. SXL 6041; London 6341.
6 Piano pieces (Ballade, intermezzi, romance) op 118:
Kempff. *With* Piano pieces op 117, op 119. SLPM 138903; DGG 138903.
Katchen. *With* Piano pieces op 117, op 119. SXL 6105; London 6404.
4 Piano pieces (Intermezzi, rhapsody) op 119:
Bishop. *With* Piano pieces op 117, Variations on a theme by Handel op 24. SAL 3758; Philips 3758.
Kempff. *With* Piano pieces op 117, op 118. SLPM 138903; DGG 138903.
Katchen. *With* Piano pieces op 117, op 118. SXL 6105; London 6404.
Vazsonyi. *With* Piano pieces op 116 nos 1-3, Variations on an original theme op 21 no 1. TPLS 13016.
4 Piano pieces op 119 no 3 only:
Curzon. *With* Intermezzo op 117 no 1, sonata 3. SXL 6041; London 6341.
Rhapsodies op 79:
Katchen. *With* Ballades op 10, Waltzes op 39. SXL 6160; London 6444.
Argerich. *Recital.* SLPM 138672.
Scherzo op 4 E flat minor:
Katchen. *With* sonata 3. SXL 6228; London 6482.

Sonatas 1 op 1 C major, 2 op 2 F sharp minor:
Katchen.   SXL 6129;   London 6410.
Sonata 3 op 5 F minor:
Curzon. *With* Intermezzi op 117 no 1, op 119 no 3.   SXL 6041;
London 6341.
Katchen. *With* Scherzo op 4.   SXL 6228;   London 6482.
Cherkassky. *With* Schubert. Piano sonata D 664.   *4FM 10012.
Variations on a theme by Handel op 24:
Bishop. *With* Piano pieces op 117, op 119.   SAL 3758;   Philips
3758.
Katchen. *With* Variations on a theme by Paganini op 35.   SXL
6218;   London 6474.
Anievas. *With* Variations on a theme by Paganini op 35.   *HQS
1028;   Seraphim S 60049.
Lympany. *Recital.*   *ST 917.
Variations on a theme by Handel op 24 (orchestrated by Rubbra):
Philadelphia Orch; Ormandy. *With* Double concerto.   SBRG
72295;   MS 7298 (*With* St Anthony variations) or M2S 686 (2 recs
With Ein Deutsches Requiem).
Variations on a theme by Paganini op 35:
Katchen. *With* Variations on a theme by Handel op 24.   SXL
6218;   London 6474.
Anievas. *With* Variations on a theme by Handel op 24.   *HQS
1028;   Seraphim S 60049.
Variations on a theme by Schumann op 9:
Katchen. *With* Variations on an original theme op 21 no 1.
Variations on a Hungarian song op 21 no 2.   SXL 6219;   London
6477.
Variations on an original theme in D major op 21 no 1:
Katchen. *With* Variations on a theme by Schumann op 9, Varia-
tions on a Hungarian song op 21 no 2.   SXL 6219;   London 6477.
Vazsonyi. *With* Piano pieces op 116 nos 1-3, Piano pieces op 119.
TPLS 13016.
Variations on a Hungarian song op 21 no 2:
Katchen. *With* Variations on a theme by Schumann op 9, Varia-
tions on an original theme op 21 no 1.   SXL 6219;   London 6477.

Waltzes op 39:

Katchen. *With* Ballades op 10, Rhapsodies op 79. SXL 6160; London 6444.

See also Piano duets p 107.

Chorale preludes op 122 nos 1 Mein Jesu, der du mich, 4 Herzlich tut mich erfreuen, 8 Es ist ein' Ros' entsprungen, 10 Herzlich tut mich verlangen:

Preston. *With* Motets. ZRG 571; ZRG 571.

Chorale preludes op 122 nos 5 Schmücke dich, O liebe Seele, 6 O wie selig seid ihr doch:

Joyce. *Recital.* *CSD 3526.

Index

No entries are included for the selected recordings of Brahms's music.

111

115

117